The Power of
VOW

The Power of
VOW

Everyday Tools for Healing

Darren Littlejohn

Rainbow Light Media
Portland, Oregon
2013

The Power of Vow
Everyday Tools for Healing

Darren Littlejohn

Cover design by Jasmine W. http://fiverr.com/jw12792
Back cover, interior layout and design by
Tamian Wood, www.BeyondDesignInternational.com
Photo by Marc Sakamoto

Rainbow Light Media
2051 SE 159th Ave
Portland, OR 97233
rainbowlightmedia.com

If you are unable to order this book from your local book-seller, you may order directly from the publisher.

Library of Congress Control Number: 2013910080
ISBN 978-0-9895260-0-5
10 9 8 7 6 5 4 3 2 1

This book is dedicated to my sister in the Dharma. She really showed me what it's like to be on this path.

"Surrender to win."
——12-Step saying

Table of Contents

Testimonials

"In Darren Littlejohn's new book, *The Power of Vow,* he writes, 'We're all addicts in a sense. We're all attached, if not addicted, to our possessions, careers, relationships, identities,' and from my own personal experience in this thing called life, I couldn't relate more. *The Power of Vow* provides readers with a concise blueprint of how to begin breaking these attachments and addictions through... you guessed it, the power of vow. I recommend this book for anyone who happens to find themselves in a human incarnation this time around."

— Chris Grosso, Author of *Indie Spiritualist Beyond Words*/Atria Books 2014

"An inspiring book: accessible and complex at the same time. I like Darren Littlejohn's integral and practical approach."

— Martine Batchelor, meditation teacher and author of *Let Go: A Buddhist Guide to Breaking Free of Habits*

"*The Power of Vow* is a must-read for everyone. Darren's straightforward approach to recovery and healing makes this book easy to read and apply to ones life."

— Brenda Feuerstein, Author and Director of Tradional Yoga Studies www.tradionalyogastudies.com

"Sadly, many well-intentioned addicts relapse. Either they didn't take their recovery seriously, or they became rigid and dogmatic about sobriety. In Darren Littlejohn's book, *The Power of Vow*, he uses the principles of Buddhism to guide addicts to the all- important middle path. By examining the difference between pain and suffering, promises and vows and finding a spiritual refuge from the turmoil of day to day life, Littlejohn provides invaluable insights for any person wishing to find meaning in life, satisfaction in spiritual practice and long term sobriety."

— Darren Main, author of *Yoga & the Path of the Urban Mystic & Inner Tranquility: A Guide to Seated Meditation*

"As a therapist I have recommended Darren Littlejohn's book *The 12-Step Buddhist* to several clients. *The Power of Vow* builds on the solid foundation of his previous book, delving deeper into Buddhist tradition and relating it to 12-Step recovery. Both books are valuable resources, especially for those who want or need to look beyond the 'God' language of 12-Step groups to access their deep healing wisdom."

— Darrell Grizzle, Ed.S. Licensed Professional Counselor

"One of the most unfortunate things that we consistently encounter in the field of chemical dependency treatment are those brilliant addicts who, based on valid experience, believe their spirituality cannot interface, thrive, blossom, and reach a greater effectiveness within the context of the 12-Step community-because of perceived religiousity. But if we study the recovery texts, we can see that they were written to invite all spiritualities, including the religion of science and of rational thought. One point turns everything on its head, and makes 12-Step recovery fundamentally pro-Buddhist. The *Alcoholics Anonymous Basic Text* says, 'With few exceptions our members find that they have tapped an unsuspected inner resource which they presently identify with their own conception of a power greater than themselves.' *The Power of Vow* helps us point to the ego as the root of the problem so that we can better tap that inner resource.

— Buster Ross, MA, CADC II, LPC-RI, Hazelden

In this important book The Power of Vow, his first after the seminal *The 12-Step Buddhist*, Darren Littlejohn drills deeper into the Buddhist path. In particular, focusing on those for whom attachment, which the Buddha identified as the root of suffering, has gone wild; a familiar condition also called addiction in the Western world. In this book Littlejohn clearly presents useful techniques and thoroughly explores the power of vow to help us all stay straight on the path.

— Michael Katz, Co-author *Dream Yoga and the Practice of Natural Light*, Author *Tibetan Dream Yoga*.

Preface

I am very happy to see Darren's new book on the power of vow. The transformative force of formally taking and holding vows is a quality that is acknowledged and utilized by many of the great religious traditions of the world. In my own Buddhist tradition it has been central from the very beginning.

The Buddha favored vows over commandments because he thought that when an individual makes a free, internal commitment to a type of ethical behavior or spiritual practice, it has a more powerful and transformative effect on the mind of that person than if they simply comply with an order made from outside. When I make a vow not to lie, for example, not only is it particularly virtuous and powerful at the moment of formally taking the vow, it has a subtle transformative power each moment that I hold that vow. And when formally taken, it can have the force of reminding me of my ethical commitment.

The Buddha taught and offered a variety of different types of vows to his disciples. Some were vows urging restraint from specific types of behaviors. For serious lay (non-monastic) Buddhist practitioners, the first five lay precepts were: restraint from killing, stealing, lying, sexual misconduct, and taking intoxicants. For ordained monks and nuns there were over 250 vows of restraint that help guide and make clear an ethical and spiritually beneficial life for those holding the vows and set a great example for the lay community for whom they represent an ideal model.

Other sets of vows were offered by the Buddha in conjunction with broader spiritual goals or in conjunction with specific advanced meditation practices. These sorts of vows often induced the cultivation of Buddha-like virtues such as compassion by urging commitments against abandoning great compassion for a single living being for even a moment. Such vows were not so much restraints on specific behaviors as much as commitments geared toward the cultivation of virtuous attitudes and mental states.

The spiritual path of a recovering addict is one where a wholesale transformation of one's ethical and spiritual center is a clear necessity. In some ways addicts and alcoholics are fortunate because of the urgency of their situation; the clarity of the suffering and the need for spiritual transformation is more readily apparent for addicts than it is for many. They understand the miserable sufferings of samsara, to use a Buddhist term. The futility of continued self-centered attitudes that are at the heart of the spiritual disease of addiction are so clearly present for an alcoholic or addict that it is difficult to deny with some semblance of self-honesty. In this sense the addict who hits bottom and begins to take steps to change their lives is fortunate.

While recognizing the misery and futility of the self-centered life of an addict is a first step in the recovery process, if it stops there, there will not be a great deal of benefit or transformation. The road ahead requires a real commitment to transformation and a willingness to do what it takes to affect that transformation. The power of vow can be an instrumental part of the spiritual path of recovery. Buddhist traditions have a great deal of wisdom to offer to many who suffer from addiction. Darren's book carries an important message that I am sure many, both inside and outside of recovery circles and Buddhist circles, will find beneficial and useful. I hope that this book on the power of vow can benefit all those who read it and put its advice into practice.

— Jim Blumenthal, Ph.D. Professor of Buddhist Philosophy at Oregon State University and Maitripa College

Acknowledgments

First of all, I owe any progress that I've ever made in understanding Dharma teachings to all of my good teachers; Chogyal Namkhai Norbu Rinpoche, Lama Zopa Rinpoche, Khachab Rinpoche, Yongey Mingyur Rinpoche, Venerable Robina Courtin, His Holiness the Dalai Lama, Joko Beck and many others. Any mistakes in this book are the fault of my own ego.

As always, Tysa Fennern is at the top of the list. She's my best friend, my biggest fan and my most stable supporter. All of the Facebook, Twitter and Google Plus friends who helped me choose the cover, edit online and who supported the self-publishing efforts on Indiegogo are too numerous to mention. But a few are Amy Asch, Tamara Lush, Mike Papas, Layna Lewis, Thomas Rozier, Matt Meinert, Meredith Obenchain, Sharon Hascall, Kevin Griffin, Brenda Feuerstein, Mary Salome, Ruth Schaefer, Chip Lechner, Ken Scott and Brita Ferm. To the anonymous donors, thank you.

Thanks to Louise Clemmer for editing above and beyond the call of duty; John Nelson for the developmental analysis; Tamian Wood for the interior and back cover layout; and Jasmine W. for the great front cover.

Thank you to all of the people who support The 12-Step Buddhist books, groups, retreats and other offerings. Without you, I wouldn't know what to write about. Thanks for helping me flesh out material time after time. It's for you. I hope you find it useful.

Author's Note

Anyone can use this book and everyone will benefit. Depending on how you want to use the book, you may want an ebook, print, or both. The print version has a workbook aspect to it. The ebook version has all of the same material, sans the pages for journaling. The material takes time to process. Feel free to take it at your own pace, alone, with a trusted individual or a study group.

Addicts especially will understand the principles because we're so deeply familiar with attachment. We're uniquely pre-qualified in our suffering to understand the teachings of the *Buddha: Awakened One*.

We're all addicts in a sense. We're all attached, if not addicted, to our possessions, careers, relationships, identities—to name a few. Everyone suffers from what Buddhists call the *Three Poisons: attachment, aversion, and ignorance*.

An attachment means that we fixate on something and fail to see what is truly happening. From a conventional sense attachment can seem harmless when we're attached to our name, gender, or material possessions. Aversion is attachment thwarted. We don't get what we want and attachment becomes aversion, such as when our lover's cute habits cease to be amusing, or when see we see things that we don't want as repulsive. Ignorance is simply not knowing something. In a Buddhist sense this means we're ignorant to our spiritual nature, and that ignorance is the root of our suffering.

Addiction is an extreme form of attachment. To me, addiction is attachment gone wild. If we're not a full-blown addict, we may easily replace the word addiction in this book with the word attachment. It works the same either way. I use the term addict to cover all addictions, physical, emotional, material, and chemical.

Aversion is another word for how we avoid unpleasantness or outright suffering. No one is capable of avoiding suffering; the key is how we individually handle our suffering. Many of us rely on our addictions to avoid suffering, which ironically leads to deeper suffering. Understanding our aversions not only helps us understand ourselves but also to heal ourselves.

Ignorance is simply a lack of knowledge and is the cause for all suffering. Understanding why, how, when, where, and even what our suffering entails, rids us not only of our own ignorance bur out own suffering.

I discuss these issues from the perspective of addiction, recovery, Buddhism, psychology, 12-Step programs, and other principles. Each of these principles spurs unique and often confusing idioms. To that end, wherever possible, I'll give simple definitions of these idioms. The first time I use a term from 12-Step, Buddhism or another place, I'll use italics, for example: *Karma: Cause and Effect.* You'll see the special term, then the everyday language of its application.

Please realize that although we're learning a term from another language, culture, and belief we're still learning it from other humans. We're all basically the same on many levels. When we accept that, we find the bridge of understanding. Rather than shut down because a term sounds unfamiliar, religious or dogmatic, we need to open our hearts, which simply leads to further understandings, teachings, and traditions from others. This is a simple way that everyone can use to understand and apply teachings from any tradition.

Hopefully this will make the material presented here simpler to digest and, most importantly, easier to use throughout our lives. If something is not clear, or we feel that a further explanation is needed please feel free to send an email to darren@the12stepbuddhist.com

Reflections

Take a few minutes to add reflections on what your Three Poisons may be:

Attachments:

_____

_____

_____

_____

_____

_____

_____

Aversions:

_____

_____

_____

_____

_____

_____

Ignorance:

_____

_____

_____

_____

_____

Sentient beings are numberless,
I vow to save them.
Desires are inexhaustible,
I vow to put an end to them.
The Dharmas are boundless,
I vow to master them.
The Buddha Way is unsurpassable,
I vow to attain it. – The Four Great Zen Vows

The 12 Steps

Adapted from Alcoholics Anonymous

Step 1: We admitted we were powerless over our addiction and our lives had become unmanageable.

Step 2: We came to believe that a power greater than ourselves could restore us to sanity.

Step 3: We made a decision to turn our will and our lives over to the care of our Higher Power as we understood our Higher Power.

Step 4: We made a searching and fearless moral inventory of ourselves.

Step 5: We admitted to our Higher Power, ourselves, and another human being the exact nature of our wrongs.

Step 6: We're entirely ready to have our Higher Power remove these defects of character.

Step 7: We humbly asked our Higher Power to remove our shortcomings.

Step 8: We made a list of all persons we had harmed, and became willing to make amends to them all.

Step 9: We made direct amends to such people whenever possible, except when to do so would injure them or others.

Step 10: We continued to take personal inventory, and when we were wrong, promptly admitted it.

Step 11: We sought through prayer and meditation to improve our conscious contact with our Higher Power, as we understood it, praying only for knowledge of our HP's will for us, and the power to carry it out.

Step 12: Having had a spiritual awakening as the result of these steps, we tried to carry this message to the addict who still suffers and to practice these principles in all of our affairs.

Principles of the 12 Steps

Step 1 Principle: Acceptance
Step 2 Principle: Confidence
Step 3 Principle: Surrender
Step 4 Principle: Self-Examination
Step 5 Principle: Self-Honesty
Step 6 Principle: Willingness
Step 7 Principle: Humility
Step 8 Principle: Forgiveness
Step 9 Principle: Restitution
Step 10 Principle: Admission
Step 11 Principle: Seeking
Step 12 Principle: Unconditional Love

Excerpts from:
The 12-Step Buddhist by Darren Littlejohn.

Why You Should Read this Book

Integration, not Separation

This book is about solving problems that cause unhappiness. It's also about integration of Buddhist principles with those from 12-Step: Alcoholics, Narcotics, Cocaine, Gamblers or Codependents Anonymous. Some of these principles are: acceptance of a problem; surrender to a higher way of thinking; and personal inventory. On their own, they can help us find relief from stress and a deeper spiritual life. But when we work with them in an integrated manner, the effects can be super-powered, allowing us to actually achieve a higher state of mind, and a new sense of aliveness.

We all learn from these teachings; even those who don't suffer from addiction or follow Buddhism. First, we need to understand some terms and their principles. It takes time, so we must be patient with ourselves. This book will show us how to use sacred vows as tools that will help us find personal power. But the power isn't the authoritarian definition. It is the influence of deep love rather than any kind of dominance over people, places, or things. It starts in our own hearts, while observing our inner thoughts, motivations, and behaviors. This insight is gained through meditation and other practices.

I've been using 12-Step programs for almost three decades. To my surprise, the vow of sobriety didn't keep me sober for life. I was sober in 12-Step programs from 1984-1994, when I relapsed and headed back to drugs and alcohol. Something was missing from my program and my spiritual journey. After 10 years sober, it was quite a shock to my psyche. I returned to recovery in 1997. At the time of this writing, I'm in my 16th year of recovery.

That's about 28 years of experience—over 25 of those years spent sober. I've been practicing meditation throughout all of those years, some more so than others. It's much easier to practice when we're not on speed and weed.

The systems of Buddhism that I've studied and practiced are mostly Zen and Tibetan. I also teach and practice Yoga, among other things. Spirituality has been a topic close to my heart since I was a boy.

This isn't a book about a new program of "Buddhist Recovery." I don't personally advocate specialized recovery programs. Recovery is recovery. But some people who are atheist, or have had difficulty with religion may have trouble feeling connected to a 12-Step culture. After all, 12-Step literature was written religious words like Father, His, God, Thee and Thou.

I think that the main author of 12-Step literature, Bill Wilson, would probably opt to change those patriarchal, religious themes with more contemporary, politically correct terminology. But Bill is no longer with us, and the literature remains somewhat archaic. The committees responsible for changes to the original books very rarely change anything. Bill W., as we've learned in the recent documentary, was an entrepreneur and a visionary. Many people in Alcoholics Anonymous had trouble with some of Bill's ideas and personal behavior. This was a constant struggle for the man. At the time he wrote the AA "big book" and, "Twelve Steps and Twelve Traditions," his work was revolutionary. But we've evolved since then.

Since the 12-Steppers seem unwilling to update the literature with better language, some of us work on this independently. I'm not personally trying to change any 12-Step program or invent a new one. Although, some people feel that's a necessity, in order to serve more addicts. I think it could help some people but is missing the point. The point is integration, not separation.

That means we should practice any teaching and participate in any program using our own knowledge as a base; instead of complaining about how they do it wrong. If we're smart, we can *integration, not separation.* understand the essence and apply it anonymously within our own hearts. Then nobody even knows the difference. We can practice our principles in harmony with anyone, anywhere. That's integration.

My hat, if I were to wear one, is off to the Buddhist Recovery Network and community for their efforts. But they've known from the beginning that my perspective is different. I'm not a fundamentalist nor am I a traditionalist. I'm an integrationist. That means I can use fundamental principles and traditions as tools for growth, without the baggage. In suffering we need a path to follow that encourages our success; that is my hope for all sufferers.

The skill of truly integrating comes in pretty handy. If we integrate principles from different systems, it follows logically that people other than those intended for the system of origin will benefit. In other words, Buddha's teachings were for the people of India over 2500 years ago. The situation was different, and the culture was quite dissimilar to today's. But the human consciousness is fundamentally not so different. That said, Buddha's teachings have evolved through other enlightened teachers over thousands of years. It's often not so much about the core of the teaching as the presentation of the principals.

The same can be said of 12-Step or any other system. It doesn't matter if the systems differ ideologically from one another. If we have a little confidence in ourselves and an open heart, we can hang with atheists and true believers at the same BBQ, without a fight. Vegans can dine with meat eaters. This is, in my non-humble opinion, revolutionary. With this thinking, it doesn't matter what our personal practice of working with a higher power is—or isn't.

In 12-Step, we're told that we're free to choose any higher power we wish. It might not be so easy, depending on where we find ourselves personally, culturally, and geographically. If anyone tells us what our higher power should be, they're more likely following the program of their ego and not that of the 12-Steps. But choosing a higher power concept is what 12-Step programs were created to do. They offer a solution, perhaps not the only solution, but a good one that works for millions.

Sometimes it seems that there really isn't much choice or that they're really just waiting for us to come around to their way of thinking. That's not within the real program. But it happens. And, addicts are also famous for finding excuses not to work within a program. We have to understand that piece as well.

However, even if we don't partici- pate in 12-Step programs, we can still benefit from the tools presented here. We can think of vows as gears to crank up our expe-

...even if we don't partici- pate in 12-Step programs, we can still benefit from the tools presented here.

rience of the promises spoken of in 12-Step litera- ture; knowing a new freedom and a new happiness that will help us to intuitively handle situations that used to baffle us. We can use Buddhist vows to make these promises a more potent reality.

Buddhist vows can be difficult to understand, especially in the context of the modern West. Most people would like to have less suffering. Few would give up their hair, clothes, and the ability to go out dancing, wear jewelry, have sex, and sleep on a nice bed. Yet those are some of the traditional rules one has to follow with their vows. There are, in fact, 253 vows for a renunciate monk and 364 for a nun. To keep all of those vows for a day is probably incred- ibly difficult.

In 12-Step we like to think of keeping our sobriety one day at a time, but in Buddhism, particularly the *Hinayana: slower, lower scope vehicle*, one has to adopt a very long-term view. The Hinayana is the path of solitary spiritual development, for the purpose of one's own enlightenment. It's said to be a small vehicle because the next one, Mahayana, includes all suffering beings in the intention. In fact, to achieve Buddhahood in the Hinayana, it takes three countless eons. What an order! Most of us would never seek enlightenment if rules like these were required to be Buddhist. Yet these are the roots of major Buddhist lineages. The good news is that we can benefit from taking vows even if we're not interested in becoming renunciate monks or nuns.

We can employ the essence of vows and apply them directly to our recovery from addictions.

I don't recommend taking vows to get clean and sober. It's best to use conventional methods like detox centers, long term treatment, and hospitals. But once some sobriety is established, probably six to twelve months at least, we can use these vows to help us find more freedom and less stress. Beyond that, we can use the vows to obtain the state of enlightenment, just like the Buddha. After all, the ultimate goal of Buddhism is to become awakened.

> *The good news is that we can benefit from taking vows even if we're not interested in becoming renunciate monks or nuns.*

I'll make the vows clear in this book so that anyone who's interested can work with them. As a non-addict, when looking through the lens of the addict, our attachments become clear—without suffering as much.

We need to know that there are conventional vows, which are more like serious promises or pledges and sacred vows. The meaning of a sacred vow is different than a promise. Once we make a vow in a spiritual context, things get more serious.

When we take a vow it's a sacred act—especially when it's done with correct understanding and intention. This is one reason why taking vows needs to be done with a clear, unintoxicated mind. Vows taken with strong awareness create a field of protection. The vow is a consecrated agreement between us and the laws of the universe. In a Buddhist sense, the sanctity of a vow isn't due to its being a promise to a God. It's more about how we raise our conscious vibration to be in tune with universal principles. We'll talk about that first.

Next we'll learn about what we need to know of karma and some other Buddhist ideas about the way life works. Then we can understand how we benefit or suffer as the result of our own actions. When we learn about karma and the many ways it comes back to us, then we take more responsibility. When we put our vows to work with an understanding of karma, they have more power. It's because if we add earnest intention with our vow, it becomes sacred. But it works in two directions.

If we change our minds and act against the vow, karma will fire back on us with what could be serious life consequences. We create an energy field that puts us in the safe space of the vow. Conversely, when we keep the vow we also keep the protection.

Addicts are no strangers to what they think are vows. We've already made a lot of them. The AA literature read aloud at meetings says that one of the many methods we've tried is swearing off forever, with and without a solemn oath. We may vow to get our drugs, we vow to get even, we vow to get the girl we want, money we need and on and on. But these are often empty promises, vacant vows. As we'll see, sacred vows are much different.

In fact, for many addicts, the idea of vowing never to touch alcohol or drugs again is laughable. We may have done it and failed miserably more than once. At Thamkrabok monastery in Thailand such a vow is a required part of their treatment for addicts. There, one has to vow never to use drugs or alcohol again for the rest of their lives just to enter their detox program. Detox at the monastery can only be done once. There is no revolving door.

To take a lifetime vow of abstinence at the beginning of our recovery is too much for many, if not most hard-core addicts. Our 12-Step method is one day at a time for a reason. When we say, "Keep coming back, it works," it's true. That said, I think that once sobriety is established, sacred vows can be extremely beneficial.

A monastery isn't necessary to practice Buddhism either. One of the problems that Westerners have with Buddhism is that it looks strange in many ways. I try to translate the meaning of *Dharma: teachings of the Buddha* about the way things are, as I've been taught from my Zen and Tibetan teachers, into practical, useful tools that can be applied to recovery. Living in a monastery, giving up sex, eating once a day, and scrubbing the floors at 4:00 AM isn't realistic or practical for many of us. Monastic life is just not my cup of Green Tea, but I respect and admire those who search for enlightenment, no matter what requirements they are forced to follow.

A monastery isn't necessary to practice Buddhism.

I discovered a trend among Western Buddhists who become monastic; they often change their minds, and then use the fact of having once been monastic as a credential to write books and teach Dharma. I'm not referring to anyone in particular. It's just that everyone who disrobes is not automatically qualified to be a Dharma teacher. In fact, the karmic bond of the vow remains, even if our integrity to the vow is lost.

The Vajrayana scriptures in the tantric path state that those who break their *samaya: tantric vows* are considered a negative influence. If vows didn't have this kind of two-way power, they would be the same as promises. We should be very mindful about taking them.

After considering some Buddhist themes we'll talk about how they relate to vows. The rest of the book will be about specific vows and how to work with them. We'll discuss purification, which helps clear up negative karma. At the end I have created a Guide for Daily Practice that can be used by groups or individuals. The importance of discovering the right path for ourselves must be our goal. I believe in deep devotion, but times have changed since the Buddha first taught. This is the modern world. We should practice Dharma in ways that make sense for us.

Reflections

What does integration mean to you?

_____

_____

_____

_____

_____

Become a Neo-Monastic

"If you don't live it, you can't give it."

While I don't feel it's necessary to become monastic in a traditional sense to practice Dharma, I am interested in the concept of the new or neo-monastic. My friend Darren Main touched on this with his book *Yoga and the Path of the Urban Mystic.*

In my view, neo-monastics are similar to 12-Step Buddhists and 12-Step Yogis. These are committed practitioners on a path. They're living in the world but are not brainwashed by the world or by spiritual paths. Neo-monastics renounce what they need when they need to, or they transform problems into solutions. All of this is done wearing street clothes, or yoga pants—without advertising it. The neo-monastic is low-key, under the radar, but working diligently to evolve. Being a neo-monastic isn't about changing the world. It's an inside job and is about directing our focus and energy on our own development.

To become a monk may be a nice idea to some addicts who like to think they're Buddhist. But if that kind of thing was a requirement to get sober I'd probably be dead by now. Maybe for some people, this kind of extreme method works and is necessary. If someone wants to go this way there's certainly nothing wrong with it. I do know of several monastics that tell me they were heroin addicts, for example. They took monastic vows, threw their lives into service, and are able to stay clean. But that's not for everyone. Twelve-Step may not be for everyone either. But I think if we can integrate the 12-Step approach with the main points of Buddhist teachings, we can become a new genre of neo-monastics.

I need the support of a local recovering community with regular meetings. *Buddhist sanghas: spiritual communities* are not the same. Addicts understand addicts

> *...if we can integrate the 12-Step approach with the main points of Buddhist teachings, we can become a new genre of neo-monastics.*

even when no one else can help. Regular 12-Step participation is something that I wouldn't want to live without. Since December 4th, 1997 I've been attending meetings. I've never felt better. But it's been a long road back to recovery for me. I have a tattoo on my arm that I got in my first year back in recovery. It says, "Magnum Iter Des Infernis," "It's a Long Way Back from Hell." To keep myself on the road of recovery, I've had to do things very differently than before. I told my whole story in *The 12-Step Buddhist*.

I didn't take the Buddhist vows until I had about eight years of clean time again. What worked for me to get my sobriety back is the vow to stay clean 24 hours at a time with the help of a sponsor, the 12 steps, meetings and a service position (making rocket fuel strength coffee). That got me into early stage recovery. But there are later stages that require more work. People in recovery often miss this piece. What worked to get us sober, works for the most part to keep us sober. But if we don't address our deeper suffering, we run the risk of relapse. Later stage recovery is a totally different level. My books are about relapse prevention and deeper recovery on one level, and the applicability of this wisdom to non-addicts on another level. Vows for me are a part of that growth. Taking vows and working to keep them while living in society is one way to practice as a neo-monastic.

Reflections

How do you feel about being a new kind of monk who lives amongst the people but doesn't display it?

_____

_____

_____

_____

_____

_____

_____

_____

_____

_____

_____

_____

Your Karma Ran Over My Dogma

Because of karma, we have contracts and connections with all of the beings who we've kept or broken promises with. Those relationships will continue in one form or another. In fact, when we recite a vow such as the one we used in our Zen training, "Sentient beings are numberless, I vow to save them all," we make contracts with all beings. All the vows we've ever made must somehow be resolved in one way or another. That may be difficult to see sometimes in our era of instant gratification. We may feel that because we were nice five minutes ago, we should never experience another moment of difficulty for the rest of our lives. But from a Buddhist perspective, our karma goes beyond one life to a number of incarnations without a beginning or an end.

We may not understand the difference between common or desperate promises, the different types of Buddhist vows and the implications of making them. We might feel that as addicts, we have no business making vows. After all, vows never kept us sober. But we don't get out of making vows if we enter a spiritual path. The vow not to vow is still a vow. We might do well to consider the power of, rather than the fear of, sacred vows. Given the context of a lifetime of broken promises, it makes sense that we'd have reservations. I hope this book guides my readers forward into a place of more confidence.

Isn't the practice of taking vows just more dogma? I used to work on dog park projects in my community. Some of the people took it pretty seriously! As a joke I used the email handle, "dogmatic" for a long time. Not everyone got it. Anyway, think about it.

Reflections

When you hear the word dogma, what do you think?

_____

_____

_____

_____

_____

_____

It's some kind of authoritarian power trip that doesn't really matter or apply to our lives. Right? Dogma is a bit of a 'you-should-do-it-this-way-or-else' kind of program. When we hear dogma we may think outdated rules, corrupt churches, hypocrites, scandals. People in recovery can be this dogmatic. They might say things like, "Work the steps or die motherfucker," or "Keep coming back," with a snicker. Incidentally, these possibly well-meaning tidbits can trigger some people with trauma in their past, delaying or ending recovery, says author Jamie Marich in her book *Trauma and the Twelve Steps*.

I've heard a lot of complaints about 12-Step dogma. People email me from all over with issues about their difficulties dealing with a conservative 12-Step mentality. They complain that their local AA group, for example, is composed of fundamentalist Bible thumpers who seem to like telling people what to do, but are clearly not the most sane or emotionally healthy people in the world.

I outlined a lot of this in *The 12-Step Buddhist* so I won't go into it much here. I always tell my readers that the best advice I can give is to quit seeking a Buddhist orientation from the meeting in North Carolina or Indiana or the Bible belt. It's better to go the traditional way, do what they say and work on Dharma privately without fighting or trying to convince people that Buddhism is better.

It takes time. But in the long run if we need to find someone else who has similar views or, once sobriety is established, maybe we can even relocate to an area with more like-minded people. The 12-Step dogma may be a pain at first, but it serves its purpose, namely, saving your ass. Not every suggestion is dogmatic and not all dogma is bad.

There's dogma that stands in the way and there are principles that can be useful. We should be able to tell the difference. But many don't even try. It's not smart to dismiss out of hand simple truths and practices just because they've been taught— if not followed perfectly—by spiritual or religious figures. That's just plain dumb. If going to church on Sunday is the folly of fools and hypocrites, so what? I'm not saying it is or isn't. But it certainly helps many people. For millions that is the core of their spirituality.

Much good comes out of these communities. For example, they give us the places where we hold

most of our 12-Step meetings! They also feed the
hungry, put clothes on kids, and build schools.
The difficulty comes from the fanatics who insist,
beyond any doubt, that their spiritual path reigns
high above everyone else's path. However, I've met
some awesome devout people. Is devotion necessary
to be moral? Not if it comes naturally.

Good people are innately good. For the rest of
us, we need all the teachings possible on how to
be virtuous. But as we say in 12-Step, we're not
bad people trying to get good, we're sick people
trying to get better. That said we do many bad
things. Moral inventory is part of step work, after
all. For those who aren't familiar, that's where we
take stock of our resentments, fears, anger, long
standing relationship difficulties, list people we've
harmed, and make amends. But by using the
disease concept, namely that we're sick-not-evil,
we overcome the dark sense of self that may keep
us stuck in addiction.

Eventually, however, the shadows must be dealt
with. Buddhist vows help with that as part of a
regular recovery program. I'm not a big fan of offering
Dharma as a substitute for 12-Step. Some people
have been trying to establish Buddhist only recovery
programs. I don't oppose efforts to help addicts get
sober. I just don't think it makes sense to split off
the recovery community into different religious
zones. My sponsor has always said that he doesn't
even agree with specialty meetings for men, women,
lawyers, etc. These may be useful for some, but I see
his point that it's supposed to be a fellowship of men
and women, not a bunch of separate tribes.

Groups tend to divide themselves into subgroups
naturally. If a separate program works for certain
individuals, then by all means use it. In my experi-

ence, both traditional and non-traditional methods are necessary. Addiction is cunning. As we say in 12-Step terms, it's the disease that tells us we don't have it. The disease, in fact, takes many forms. The Addict within knows how to shape-shift. It doesn't really care what we're addicted to; sex, money, guns, video games, bacon cheeseburgers. As long as we're soaking in attachment, the Addict is running the show.

The non-addict doesn't have the same kind of problem at the same level of intensity. We all have attachment. But addiction is attachment gone wild. It's all the way on the other end of the continuum— but it's on the same continuum.

When we call something dogmatic, are we rebelling against authority, or just trying to weasel our way out of doing something that requires hard work and discipline? Just because we don't understand foreign terms, does that mean that we should automatically reject the message? Sometimes I think that people in general and addicts in particular miss the point. I often say, don't throw the Buddha out with the bathwater. That means we shouldn't focus too much on the message delivery system; people, books, institutions, and miss the awesomeness of the message.

> *don't throw the Buddha out with the bathwater.*

The 12-Step literature says, "Be quick to see where religious people are right." But most of the time all we can talk about is how wrong they are. This is the Victim archetype. It works with the Saboteur archetype to keep us from changing. The ego is afraid of change. Not to be trite but as we say in meetings, if nothing changes, nothing changes. It means that if we don't change our behavior and attitude, we won't get different results.

In the Dharma, we study the reality of change, called *impermanence: everything changes*. Nothing exists as it appears. It's better if we can see this. To see it we calm our minds—we don't shut them off. To calm our minds we reduce our problems. Vows help us reduce problems by reminding us of what our behavior should or shouldn't be. This is one way of looking at it and the way we'll be talking about the path in this book.

There are other views besides renouncing everything. The point is that we can find the truth in what might appear to be dogma. Don't reject the teaching because of the packaging. Try not to be afraid of doctrine. If we want to rebel against something, we must bypass the rigidity of our own ignorance. These ancient tools are powerful—they create Buddhas. In the long run, addicts are no different than non-addicts. This is probably more difficult for non-addicts to understand than addicts. Addicts use the severity of their situation to understand and apply Buddha's teachings. Non-addicts may have to meditate for decades or face a life altering situation, or both, to crack open the ego enough to gain this kind of insight. That's my bias, because I'm an addict, and a Buddhist, and a 12-Step Buddhist. That doesn't mean I'm an atheist or anti-theistic. Some teachers seem to make it their mission to reject what they call the theistic approach to 12-Step recovery. There is no need to reject anything if we understand Dharma correctly.

Even the nicest, smartest people can use some guidelines. Take a look at the world. It seems that even with all of the spiritual teaching out there, we're still at each other's throats. Because of this, many people in recovery like to say, "I wish the rest of the world were in recovery so they'd be spiritual, like us." Addicts have this tendency to see themselves as different. There's a lot of evidence to support that. But good people don't need a lot of rules, or "suggested steps." They just do the right thing because it's the right thing. Right? Some—maybe all—of us could use a long look at the advice given by spiritual traditions and try to find the useful tools available to us.

Fear of work on one hand and traditionalism on the other are also issues in Buddhism. In the West, we can be a little entitled and ethnocentric to the extent that we shun what we don't understand. Some people get uncomfortable at a Dharma center, for example. Some are inspired. But we all have to make it past the strange things being said in different languages. We might be confused when we show up to learn meditation and are confronted with images of deities on fire or statues of Dharma protectors that look more like demons than monks.

Because of this, some people want to water Dharma down so much that it loses some of its meaning and most of its potency. Others won't listen to any Western teachers because they don't feel they are legit. The number of books on mindfulness has grown tremendously in the past decade. But it seems to me that there's a lot of rehashing of the same basic ideas.

My Facebook Profile Says
I'm Buddhist

It's easy to think we're Buddhist because we've learned a little about how to be mindful. Mindfulness is being present to what is happening in the moment as opposed to the past or future. There are many levels of mindfulness and many subtle layers to become mindful of. The tantric teachings of Hinduism, Yoga, Vajrayana Buddhism, Bon and other systems teach us about these subtle energies.

Mindfulness is a magical tool. But just because we're aware that we're spreading almond butter on our gluten free toast instead of thinking about paying our bills, doesn't mean we're enlightened— yet. Basic mindfulness, such as focus on the breath or body sensations, is just a beginning. Yet it seems that in the mainstream all we can talk about is this intro level stuff. After a while, deeper understanding is needed. That means deeper commitment that yields more powerful results.

The Buddha gave us strong medicine because we have a pretty tricky disease, namely the belief that we exist. It's called "False Evidence Appearing Real, F.E.A.R." The world looks solid, permanent, and concrete—in many ways. We think of ourselves in this way. We defend our right to be right, our money, property and prestige. But none of it is real. Nothing is as it appears to our minds.

When we mistakenly think a little mindfulness once in a while is enough to penetrate the karmic density built up over eons, we might want to look a little further. If plaque buildup on our teeth can get bad, think about the reinforcement of cosmic delusion that can build up over a few trillion life-times. It takes a Buddha Powered Sonicare and a team of karmic purification-hygienists to clean up the mess. But many teachers in the West seem to keep the message so light duty that it doesn't even tap the truth. It's like using a toothpick to dig out a rotten tooth. Who knows, maybe they're trying to make money, collect followers, and build themselves up. It's a little like being a politician. We try to be Centrist to avoid marginalizing our base. I'm not like that. Maybe I'm a little more of a Buddhist Ralph Nader. I don't get as many votes, but the people who listen not only agree but also understand. I'm not trying to be political here either; this is just an example.

> *Nothing is as it appears to our minds.*

There's a similar situation in popular, Western yoga. There's Buddha Dharma, Yoga Dharma and many others. But in the Buddhist Dharma, some teachers try to preach about how they're not preachy. Their marketing pitch is that there's no dogma. But there's always someone getting paid and that is the one everybody listens to. Many people are looking for authority to follow and that breeds dogma. It's fascinating how some teachers can act puritanical about the "real" Buddhism—as if there's only one legitimate view—then immediately refer to themselves as radical and revolutionary. It's a contradiction. Can we really have it both ways? Can we say, we're dogma free, and at the same time reject the authenticity of other traditions? That's actually very preachy.

When we extract the essence of the various practices, we can mix it up. Perhaps we sing in the Gospel choir, get a Green Tara tattoo, hang out in a sweat lodge—without judgment. Then we're really being non-dogmatic. That's called integration. When we practice this way maybe we can connect the dots a little. We might put together our own meaningful life changing, transformative, awesome practices that aren't limited to a school, a tradition or a single teacher.

Conversely, we could also stay committed to a single school, meditation method and instructor. We can go either way. That's the beauty of integration. It's especially cool if we can get the Teaching without being brainwashed. It takes guts and it takes the ability to think for oneself. Now that shit is revolutionary. It's punker than punk. It takes a certain level of composure and flexibility and freedom to work with spiritual teaching however it appears to us.

Some people are dogmatic. Fine. Some are anti-anything new. No problem. It's all part of the evolution of consciousness. It's natural that people tend to protect what they think they own. Good ideas are so hard to come by. It's no wonder that thinkers tend to build schools around them and defend their honor to the end.

Reflections

What does being Buddhist mean to you?

_____

_____

_____

_____

_____

_____

_____

Popeye and the Buddha Walk Into a Bar

Here's a note on style. I often say things that rattle cages. If that happens, please feel free to move on to something else. Otherwise, I invite you to join me on the path of serious self-inquiry that has occupied most of my life. As we say in the programs, take what you want, leave the rest.

I am what I am. Some people read to learn. Some people read to refute. My style is my own. Some people like it, others don't. I have a tendency to be a little sharper edged than some feel-good-Buddhist writings. There's nothing wrong with feeling good. But in my experience as an addict in and out of recovery, the thrust to feel something other than what I'm feeling has played a big role in keeping me hooked in a cycle of suffering. If you want to heal the pain you've got to feel the pain. If you know another way, then by all means, pursue it. On the other hand, I don't make any special effort to make things blunter than they need to be. But I don't try to soften the blow of reality as I see it. For those who prefer an easier, softer style, there are plenty of other resources. The neo-monastic tells it like it is.

There is nothing definitive about this work or any other. There is no "universal rule" that works for all people in all times and places. The sutras and tantras, monastic codes and lay codes for moral behavior in Buddhism vary from tradition to tradition—with some strong common ground among these as well as some disagreement. In this book, I'll offer practices based on similarities, as I've understood them. Keep in mind that understanding, too, is subject to change. In recovery we often say that to follow a program using spiritual principles is simple but not easy. Ethical decisions made in light of Buddhist precepts can be complex. Some sources contradict each other. We should have clear reasons to commit to a path and that takes deep thought.

My intention is to be of benefit. The inertia that keeps us spiritually stuck is a form of cosmic laziness. We don't see the forest through the trees and perhaps we don't even know we're in the forest. Many of us are too busy daydreaming that we're in the tropics sipping Margaritas with impunity. I'm as guilty of this as anyone—if not more so. The methods that I talk about are based on what works for me. I didn't invent any of it. It's all interpretation.

> *If you want to heal the pain you've got to feel the pain.*

Any mistakes made in presenting Dharma that deviate from in the original intent of the teachings I have received is a result of my own ignorance. Interpretations change in time and with practice. Buddha taught impermanence. Everything changes, especially our knowledge of the real meaning of Dharma. That said; take what you want, and leave the rest. I do my best to explain Dharma the way that it works for me. My way of approaching recovery, namely in a comprehensive, multi-faceted, no-holds-barred, dynamic manner, keeps me alive. I like alive. It beats the alternative. And it keeps me out of the Funnel.

Reflections

What would you like to keep and what would you discard from this section or the book so far?

_____

_____

_____

_____

_____

_____

Get Through the Funnel

Sometimes in recovery we hit a wall. My *sponsor: 12-Step mentor*, John P., calls it the 'Funnel.' The Funnel is a symbol for the decrease in numbers of people who get sober, compared to those who are sober a number of years. Many people get sober, fewer stay and fewer still remain long term. If we observe sobriety birthday countdowns in a 12-Step meeting, we'll see that the wide end of the Funnel is composed of people in early sobriety. Then the Funnel narrows. As we go up in years, we go down in numbers. Thus, the physical example of the Funnel fits that pattern.

The Funnel is also a way to describe the narrow black hole that we sometimes find ourselves in. Sobriety—life itself—becomes boring, stagnant, and repetitive. We may wonder why we don't just get loaded. We can get depressed, or worse. We may seek stimulation in the form of other addictions. I didn't make it through the Funnel my first time in recovery. After 10 years clean I slipped through the cracks.

For the non-addict, the Funnel can be a sense of meaninglessness, existential distress, mid-life crisis, or long-term illness or depression. No one is exempt. We can all wind up in a place where we wonder what the point is. Sometimes we can get stuck there.

To get out of the Funnel we usually need a drastic life change of some kind. Relapse can happen at any stage of recovery. One of the biggest causes is failure to deal with our family of origin issues and other past traumas. Long term, healthy sobriety often requires a personality reintegration and some major shifts in lifestyle.

When I meet people who seem like they're in the Funnel I often recommend that they take up an extreme solution, such as training for a marathon, going to grad school, becoming vegan or a hot yoga instructor. The first time I went through the Funnel—with around a decade of sobriety—I relapsed. The second time I took Buddhist Vows. I think they work pretty well. The next time I need a radical shift to get out of the Funnel I might become a ski instructor, or an acrobat.

Reflections

Have you or someone you've known ever been in the Funnel? What was it like?

_____

_____

_____

_____

_____

_____

_____

Opening Meditation

The purpose of the following meditation is to set our intention before we delve into the material. This meditation goes beyond a *4th step inventory: self-examination step from the 12-Steps,* or an *8th step list: a list of those we have harmed.* The intention is to acknowledge everyone we've ever connected with in this life, and in every life we've ever lived.

The sky before me is filled with radiant Buddhas. Blessings pour from the hearts of all Awakened Ones to all beings in my time-space network.

My intention for doing any kind of practice is to be of maximum benefit, and to end suffering for others and myself. It is to heal wounds, no matter how old. I'm karmically connected to all of my relations, from time without a beginning. Every association that I've ever had is included in my meditation. I send healing light to all. It radiates from my heart chakra: energy portal. As I meditate, faces and feelings arise in my mind-stream: ongoing consciousness from this lifetime and others. I hold the intention to heal each one. Everyone who I've ever helped—or harmed—is drenched with healing light beams of all colors.

These scenes fill me with hope and a new vision. With this clarity, I relax into a state of relative compassion for myself, and others. I think about the six realms, which will be discussed in detail. In every realm where I've been, in whatever form, I have made connections; good and bad. The bills are past due. One day, when the conditions are correct, all karmas will ripen: seeds will bear fruit. Every time I feel a strong reaction with someone, it's because of our past karma; my actions, my intentions, my results. These relationships can and will be purified with my practice. With the power of my intention and meditation, with the power of Healing Buddhas, I send the light of compassion to all beings. May all of these relationships be made right.

Why Vow?

The Four Noble Truths

This is my interpretation. Translations and presentations of these vary.

Life is suffering.

Suffering has a cause.

Different causes create different results (happiness instead of suffering).

Here's how: **The Noble Eightfold Path**; right view, intention, speech, livelihood, effort, mindfulness, concentration and action. These good causes yield a calm mind and good conditions for practice.

Suffering and its Causes

When we understand the types of suffering that exist, we can do something about them. We might take a vow, such as the vow not to harm, because we understand that we suffer on different levels.

The Buddha taught the Four Noble Truths. The first of these is that life is suffering. It's not meant to be pessimistic. Buddha kept it real. We suffer because we get what we want and it doesn't last. We suffer because we don't get what we want. In the material world, there are no gains that can completely liberate us from our sorrow. Sometimes people tell me that they're grateful for their suffering. It teaches them. It's true, we can learn from our suffering. Since we're suffering, we might as well try to find an upside. But Buddha talked about a path out of suffering.

We like some things and become attached to them. We reject other things and try to avoid them. We're not aware of this process or the real pure nature that is our secret identity in which this process occurs.

We suffer when we get a little bump on the head. That's the suffering of suffering. We also suffer when things change. This is called the suffering of change.

We get a good feeling, but it doesn't last. We find the perfect lover—they find someone else. We're young and virile, and then we get old and flabby. Any time, without warning, we can be healthy, and then get sick. We can be alive, then not. It's all very tenuous, and thinking about it gives most of us anxiety. But Buddhism asks us to do just that.

We get used to the way things are and we identify with the people, places and things in our lives and with ourselves. These things never stay the same. Neither do we. Change comes hard for addicts. We say we want it, and then we don't know what to do with it. Somehow through our Buddhist practice we can learn to be Present (with a capital P) as everything in our life changes.

There's a deeper suffering than either of these. This is called pervasive suffering. This is the underlying suffering, the anxiety, and the fear that pervades our existence. It usually sits just beneath the surface of our awareness. When we do step work, therapy, meditate or practice *hatha: physical, movement based or other yoga techniques*, such as ethics, meditation, visualization sometimes stuff comes up. We may not even know what we're feeling or why we're feeling it. Trauma is often buried deep in our bodies and our psyche.

For addicts in early sobriety we're confronted will all kinds of feelings, responsibilities, previously blotted out memories. Meditation is like that. We can come to understand and even tolerate this pervasive suffering. It takes guts, for example, to be at one with the underlying, acute sense of our own imminent death. Who wants to be aware of that? Mostly nobody. But those with intelligence, mettle and determination will learn to face it instead of seeking endless distractions. Or at least we can learn to face pervasive suffering a little bit—in between distractions.

Sometimes we suffer a little, sometimes a lot. However we try to soothe ourselves, we still wind up needing more balm—whatever forms the balm be it drugs, food, sex, people, concepts, or thrills. When we live in ignorance of the patterns of attachment, ignorance and hatred, there's no end in sight to the struggle to become happy and pain free.

Reflections

What are your feelings about suffering?

_____

_____

_____

_____

_____

_____

One reason that we might need vows is to end this suffering caused by desire. We can meditate on our situation in what is called the desire realm. That's one of the realms of samsara: *the infinite cycle of birth, sickness, old age, death, and rebirth.* There are sub realms within the desire realm. These are the dimensions in which all sentient beings are said to *transmigrate: cycle through endlessly, one rebirth at a time.*

As humans, we are said to live in the human dimension of this desire realm. It's called the precious human rebirth because, though it's wrought with sufferings, this dimension affords us the opportunity to break free from the infinite cycle of endless sufferings. One text offers a way to meditate on the undesirability of the desire realm. Have a deep breath before you read this one:

"Not only do the beings of the Desire Realm engage in [these] bad activities; they also have great suffering. At the time of birth, they undergo the suffering of birth; then they undergo the sufferings of aging, sickness, and death. They also undergo the sufferings of separation from the pleasant and meeting with the unpleasant. They lack what they want and must seek it with great exertion and fatigue; they have to engage in many types of work— road building, the manufacture of iron, carpentry— and once they have achieved what they want. They have to maintain it; as soon as we leave the house, we have to lock the door. There is also the suffering of not knowing satisfaction with what we have.

Further, there is the suffering of lacking independence; though we achieve what we want and maintain it, we cannot use it as we wish. Sometimes, even when we can use something as we wish, it causes trouble, as when we cannot digest food. There are many cases of not being able to enjoy what we use, for example, having a thick coat but getting too warm in it, or getting cold from wearing a thin garment. There is also the suffering of losing friends and mates: boyfriends lose girlfriends and girlfriends lose boyfriends. Even these sufferings would be bearable, but the beings of the Desire Realm also have the suffering of a short lifespan, as well as the suffering of sleep, which is a fault.

As for resources in the Desire Realm, the beings use impure substances for nourishment; moreover, there are impure substances such as urine and feces that do not exist in the First Concentration. This is how we contemplate the faults of Desire Realm beings." -*Meditative States in Tibetan Buddhism*

We're said to move from realm to realm for infinity. This is what is meant by transmigration. We move through six different dimensions, called the six *lokas* of the desire realm:

God Realm
Jealous God Realm
Human Realm
Animal Realm
Hungry Ghost Realm
Hell Realm

Each of these realms has its characteristics. There are subdivisions, such as the many levels of hot and cold hells. There are many books and teachings given on this topic. I've spent whole retreats learning about and meditating on these six realms. It's not important to dwell on it morbidly. What good is our practice if it makes us neurotic? But if we can get a sense of how our actions cause suffering, we have motivation to change the actions from bad to good.

The hell realm is a place of infinite, unbearable sufferings. In the hungry ghost realm we thirst forever and if we find a sip of water, our throats are too tiny to drink. Most addicts understand this one. The animal realm is one of paranoid survival where we hunt and are hunted endlessly. Just watch the

> *Gods exist in the desire realm and, in Buddhist cosmology are not considered enlightened beings.*

Discovery Channel for examples. We may like to romanticize the natural world of animals but it's quite brutal. The human realm is where we have the chance to hear the Teachings of a Buddha, get on the path to end suffering and rebirth into lower realms. The Jealous God realm is one where we live for thousands of years as beings more powerful than humans. But we fight and kill each other because of our ignorance, fear of losing what we have or not getting what we want. It's like a crazy Titan Town. In the God realm, we're so cracked out on power and apparent freedom from sufferings that we don't see a need to practice a spiritual path. After all, we're Gods. Gods exist in the desire realm and, in Buddhist cosmology are not considered enlightened beings. When we're in this realm we eventually burn out our good karma and return to a lower realm.

Reflections

What do you feel when you think about these different realms?

Hell Realm

_____

_____

_____

_____

Hungry Ghost Realm

_____

_____

_____

_____

Animal Realm

_____

_____

_____

_____

Human Realm

_____

_____

_____

_____

Jealous God Realm

_____

_____

_____

_____

God Realm

_____

_____

_____

_____

For our purposes it's important to know that all of these realms are about suffering. We take vows to be on the path to end suffering. Our negative actions can cause us to experience greater suffering than we can imagine. In the human realm, we can see how much suffering exists. In the lower realms, it's worse. We want to avoid lower rebirths into these realms. The best option, according to the teachings, is to be reborn in a good human situation. This way we can continue to meditate, study, and practice the path of enlightenment. I have heard it said that Buddha gave teachings in the God realm. There it might be possible to be on the path. But mostly the Lamas say that the human realm is the realm of choice for practice because we can have the clarity and the movitation to be on the path.

This is important because we need to understand that we have the ability to end suffering in this human dimension. We have the ability to examine our situation truthfully, admit our defects and make new choices. That's what the 12 Steps, and the Noble Eightfold Path are all about.

It begins with 'right view,' which is about understanding our condition. We can see through, study, and practice that the conventional view of suffering is normally that it's not our fault. We know in our 12-Step work that we have to own our own responsibility for the situation we have and the effects that our behavior has had on others. That's a big part of working a 12-Step program. The right view in Buddhism is also about understanding that everything that arises, arises from a cause. We see that cause and we can make new choices. The view is also about emptiness: the unreal nature of everything. There are many books and teachings on emptiness. We won't go into much detail here, except to say that nothing is as it appears. Nothing is as we think it is. Everything is, as Buddha said, unreal. Just like a dream. This one takes a bit of work to wrap our minds around. But it's essentially the first main realization in Buddhism. When we realize emptiness, we've come a long way towards enlightenment. Emptiness is a big part of the 'right view.' But it's an advanced topic.

We also have 'right intention' to work with. We can ask ourselves why we're doing what we're doing. In 12-Step, we often call this checking our motives. Karma, as we'll discuss below, accumulates with three conditions: intention, action and satisfaction.

Everything is, as Buddha said, unreal. Just like a dream.

When we have the right intentions, for example to be of benefit to others or to find compassion in our own hearts, then we accumulate some good karma with our actions. But we also get points for rejoicing in those actions.

We can say a lot about 'right speech.' But if we have the right view and understand that our behavior affects us, and those around us, we can speak in a manner that serves, rather than causes more problems. We can also think about using sacred *mantra: a blessed verbal formula repeated in prayer, meditation, or incantation* as right speech. There are an infinite number of things we can choose to do differently with some awareness. How we write emails, post messages on Facebook, argue with people on political points, and work to get our own satisfactions met are all subjects that are eligible for right speech practice.

'Right livelihood' means that our work is about compassion and service, rather than greed and pollution and other negative elements. This is an area that can be difficult to manage for addicts in sobriety. Many of us have learned to survive by the hustle. We work in bars, as drug dealers, strippers, sex workers, shady sales positions. It often takes a big adjustment to switch into right livelihood. Of course, non-addicts can benefit as well from choosing a vocation or at least a manner of working that has good benefits for others. Our vows will help us work with this, and all of the principles of the Noble Eightfold Path. What we're talking about now is really the foundation for knowing why we would take vows. For example, if we vow not to cause harm, and our job causes harm, then we break our vow. That breaks our commitment to ourselves to become free of suffering and achieve total liberation for the benefit of all beings.

All of our efforts should be fueled by all of the principles we discuss here. We have to work at this to create change. It's not so easy for most of us and it doesn't come naturally for addicts especially. Knowing that it's going to take effort on the path is key to being successful. Just like going to the gym or practicing any kind of physical health program, we have to work past the inertia that keeps us stuck. When we apply such effort with the right views, right intentions, right speech, and right livelihood, we accumulate the power of good karma. Vows protect us. Vows are self-fulfilling prophecies. When we make and keep vows always working toward this under-standing we build ourselves a Dharma Fortress.

Of course all of this kind of work requires us to be able to practice mindfulness. Most people underes-timate the power of deep mindfulness. I've said this in my groups and retreats many times. If we're really practicing mindfulness, we can see everything. It's easy to trick ourselves into thinking we're spiritual or

Buddhist or something because we meditate, move a little slower, talk a little quieter, and eat vegetarian. But we're really trying to establish the mindfulness of the Buddha, who *was omniscient: infinite knowledge, awareness, understanding, insight or perception.* Does that mean that Buddha was also *omnipotent: infinite power, authority, and might?* No. He learned to master his own unique dimension and to teach others about the path. But let's keep it real; mindfulness is an infinite practice.

Part of the skill that we develop with meditation and study is that of concentration. We can practice single-pointedly until we can sit for hours, or longer, in seated meditation in an undistracted manner. There are levels upon levels of this type of skill. Many systems offer comprehensive instruction and support on just this aspect of being Buddhist. It relates to vows because if we're not able to focus we can't be aware of the subtle levels of view, intention, speech, livelihood and action. We must develop a focused, discriminating awareness in order to master our own dimensions, like the Buddha. But let's not make concentration the end game. It is a requirement on the path, but is not sufficient to liberate us, or anyone else, from suffering. After all, addicts can have pretty good concentration skills as they're seeking, acquiring, and using drugs. All of the principles of the Noble Eightfold Path work together. It matters what we're concentrating on, how we concentrate and what we do with the insights that we gain from perfecting concentration. Right actions are those that bring merit and reduce suffering. If we live with these eight in mind, we have plenty of work to do to stay present on the path of liberation. It's not easy, but the power of vow supports our practice in all of these ways.

The Four Foundations of Mindfulness

There are infinite things to be mindful of. When we meditate or practice Dharma, we put our minds on virtuous topics. To meditate on the four mindfulness topics of karma, impermanence, samsara, or precious human rebirth is an excellent way to practice. These following four concepts are also indispensable to understanding Buddhist thought. They are sometimes presented in a different order. It isn't really necessary to learn them in order. It's not like a linear process.

The Tibetan Master Longchenpa once said that to know one is to know all. In my experience, the understanding of karma came easily. Impermanence made sense intellectually but took more time to develop a deeper, experiential knowledge. Since I've lost several friends in the past few years, the meditation on just how precious our short time as humans can be

...meditate on the four mindfulness topics of karma, impermanence, samsara, or precious human rebirth

comes naturally. The suffering of samsara is every-where, all of the time—if only we choose to look.

The point of working with these principles is to really learn what mindfulness is all about as it pertains to understanding our situation in samsara. If we don't see a problem, we have no motivation to find a solution. Sometimes we lie to ourselves and we don't even know it. These tools can help us get real about what is what. There are more books than ever before written on mindfulness. Remember, anything can be the object of meditation. When we apply these principles as they relate to vows, we can establish, develop and maintain an understanding of why we benefit from vows. It takes an open mind and some time to develop our understanding of Dharma on a deep level. My advice is to let the door open. The light will shine in and go into our hearts. When we practice with this kind of openness, every-thing in our situation changes.

Karma: Cause and Effect

This is a very brief overview of karma in the simplest terms. Karma is considered to be a law. But it's the law that we can't break. It will work for us or against us—but it always works. If we know how it works, we can use it to our advantage. We chalk up karma points with good deeds and we wipe out our merits with dirty deeds, whether they're done dirt cheap or not. Intention plays a big role in karmic potential. Situations are complex. There is no such thing as a single cause to any event. Time is infinite. One event can lead to infinite results. When we think like this, it's not always 100% cut and dried to figure out what's best. In the long run, what seems to be a negative might turn out to be a positive. The example I always use for this is the day I got sober. It seemed like a bad day. But with the intention to stop suffering, the action of going to a meeting and the satisfaction with a day of clean time, things turned out better. Then I relapsed. Was it bad karma? It felt bad. Now I'm in a place I wouldn't be if that hadn't happened.

Reflections

What seemed to be a negative, but turned out to be a positive in your life?

_____

_____

_____

_____

_____

_____

_____

_____

We do our best to use guidelines like those found in the 12 Steps, Buddhism, and other spiritual systems. On a recent retreat I mentioned to my teacher that I was making mistakes, but was doing my best. He looked at me and said, "That's all we can do. If we do our best, then there is no problem." Good enough!

From a 12-Step Buddhist perspective, when we screw up, the Dharma Police aren't going to give us a fine. Buddha's not watching with a scorecard. There is no judge in the sky handing out punishments. The karmic potential, however, adds up. To practice with karma means full ownership, total freedom and utter responsibility. It's the most basic of concepts that must be understood if we're to enter the path of Buddhism. If someone says they're Buddhist but they don't believe in karma, in my opinion they're not Buddhist. They're something, but not Buddhist.

Karma is a notion that was already well known in India at the time of the historical Buddha. But the explanations in other systems, such as Hinduism led to different conclusions. In Buddhism, and most other systems that I've encountered, karma means action.

The law of karma means that every action has a cause. Whatever we experience, good or bad, is the result of past intentions, actions and satisfactions. We do positive things, and we get positive results. When we do negative things, we get those negative results. But not all positive or negative actions bear the same type of fruit. The Dharma teachings explain in great detail how this works. But for many of us, it's difficult to understand karma because we lose track of the infinite storehouse of

> *Whatever we experience, good or bad, is the result of past intentions, actions and satisfactions.*

karmic seeds that make up our existence. It takes high levels of meditative realization to see things like this. These seeds are like potentialities that can become activated when secondary conditions appear. It's like the seed of an oak tree sitting in the dirt. If there's no water, heat, light, nutrients, there's no oak tree. A seed may lie dormant for a very long time until the right conditions make it possible to sprout. But like any seed that's buried, it's easy for us to forget that it's there. Yet the potentiality remains.

It may be hard for us to understand the karmic time delay. Most people can't see into the past, present and future all at once. Karma isn't always instant, no matter what John Lennon said. It can happen that way, of course. But for a karmic seed to ripen, three things are required: intention, action and satisfaction. Because of this, there are differences in how and when karma ripens. For example, if we kill without intention, we don't really create much negative karma. If we step on a bug without seeing it, we don't have the intention to cause harm. Because we didn't have the intention, we don't have the satisfaction either. Without the second and third factors of intention and satisfaction, the karmic seed created isn't infused with the same potentiality. If we find a mosquito on our neck and smack it with the intention to kill, we create the next level of potentiality, that of intention. If we take pleasure in the action and relish in it after, we're in all the way. We've created a negative seed that will ripen when the conditions for sprouting are ripe.

> *. . . for a karmic seed to ripen, three things are required: intention, action and satisfaction.*

But are we stuck with our karma once we've created it? If we kill with intention, but later realize that we made a mistake, we can purify our karma. We'll talk later about some methods of purification that we can find in different systems of Buddhism.

Some Buddhists have a tendency to think that once the seeds are sown, our karma is permanently set. Whatever the situation, they say, "Well that's your karma." If you can't get a job, that's your karma. If you get sick, that's your karma. It's true, but sometimes we miss the fact that karma can be purified. If karma could not be purified, we'd all be screwed. There has to be a chance to clean it up, otherwise how would we ever fully realize our true

Buddha nature? The logic isn't hard to understand. If sentient beings live without the spiritual knowledge of karma and its potentiality for infinite lifetimes, we accumulate negativity based on our attachment, ignorance and aversion—ad infinitum. Not knowing that we are the creators of our own misery, we take what we want, fulfilling the karma of attachment. We allow ourselves to feel hate, act on it and thus create more and more negativity. Ignorant of the potentiality of accumulating positive merit, we fail to practice generosity, patience, compassion. It's not hard to see that we just dig ourselves deeper and deeper into the hole of negative karma. But it is hard to apply this knowledge!

We can also collect positive karma to outweigh the negative. Perhaps the positive neutralizes the negative somehow or at least keeps us in circumstances where the negative doesn't meet conditions of ripening. This is normally spoken of as the accumulation of merit. If we're fortunate enough to receive the teachings of Buddha or from later teachers who've taught on karma, we may realize that we should collect positive karma; will we ever be able to accumulate enough positive to overcome the entire negative? Think about the potentiality of infinite beings creating infinite sufferings in infinite ways throughout beginningless time.

We perform one negative action. Perhaps we harm another being. That being responds with a negative action to another being, which responds to another. All of the beings that respond to suffering by creating more suffering perpetuate suffering infinitely. It just goes on without end. One negative action, especially when fused with intention and satisfaction, has infinite possibility to create endless suffering. A vast storehouse of karma can build up over time. Since time is infinite, causes and effects are infinite, karma is infinite and suffering is infinite.

How many good deeds would it take to clean it up? That would be a Ninth Step of epic proportion. It would be possible, if we take vows, restrain our negative proclivities, meditate and accumulate for a very, very long time. If we create ten million positive actions and only two hundred thousand negatives, eventually we could wind up on top of the karma game. But how long will it take? And do we have the discipline required to make it happen? It seems impossible. Talk about, "What an order, I can't go through with it!" But we can. And vows are an important tool that we can use. The vow actually perpetuates accumulation of positive karma—when we keep the vow. Conversely, when we break it, the cost is higher than if we did not have a vow. That's why we have purification practices.

> *Since time is infinite, causes and effects are infinite, karma is infinite and suffering is infinite.*

If you're still curious you can attend some live or webcast retreats with the Dalai Lama or another great teacher. Also read my first book, or make a study of thick volumes such as Karma: Steps on the Path to Enlightenment: A Commentary on Tsongkhapa's Lamrim Chenmo, Vol 2: Karma by Geshe Sopa.

This is the way I look at karma. You may disagree. Perhaps your teacher explains it another way. That's fine. Meditate on it and learn to fine tune your own understanding. All I can share with you are the teachings I've received and the understanding that I've come to over the years. It might look different down the road. Everything changes.

Reflections

Explain karma to a two year old.

_____
_____
_____
_____
_____
_____
_____
_____
_____
_____
_____
_____
_____
_____
_____
_____
_____
_____
_____
_____
_____

Impermanence: Change

Buddha called the fact that everything changes impermanence. By everything, we mean everything. There is not one single atom in the universe that is fixed, permanent, concrete or, as some Buddhists say, inherently existent from its own side. Because we understand something of karma, we can trace any object, thought, or other phenomena from its current state to its previous state or the state the situation was in before the cause created the effect. Take a glass of water for example. There it is, sitting in front of us. How'd it get there? We went to the cabinet, grabbed a glass, and filled it up. It came from some store perhaps, before that a manufacturer, before that perhaps it was sand, before that who knows? Some elements make up the molecular structure of sand. Where did those molecules come from? Can we find their beginning? What about the water? Trace it back, and back, and back. Nothing stays in its current state. Nothing just popped up out of nowhere in its current state. Causes are always preceded by causes. We can examine through a multitude of methods how everything in the phenomenal world, the world of samsara, is impermanent.

There's the question of how things in the universe come into existence. And there's the question of how they cease to exist in the form that we think they exist. Energy never dies; it only changes into different states. The point is that nothing stays the same. In 12-Step language we say that this too, shall pass. Buddhism calls it impermanence. But knowing this intellectually is of limited value. Somehow we have to take this experience into our meditation, and bring our meditation into our experience. In a sense we can realize impermanence, just like we can have realizations on any of the other teachings.

Remember, if we think we understand it, we don't understand it. It's not what we think. Thinking is a construct, an after effect, a label, a tool. It's not the ultimate knowledge. That's not to say that we should give up thinking. We have brains for a reason. The human form is designed with the capacity to liberate ourselves from suffering. Reptiles can't think about their lives because they have no cerebral cortex. But we can! That means we have to be able to think straight. How can we practice good view, intention, and satisfaction if we don't think clearly? The vows, meditations and practices of Buddhism and the 12 Steps help us think more clearly.

The vows, meditations and practices of Buddhism and the 12 Steps help us think more clearly.

People in 12-Step recovery often struggle with this idea. They say we're not supposed to think too much. I get the same impression from a lof of Zen practitioners. But with Buddhist tools, we refine our thinking. We develop, evolve, and understand on an intellectual level that nothing is as it appears;

nothing stays the same. It's a big part of getting into a good meditation space. That, in turn, helps us act more mindfully and live more fully. Vows help remind us of all of these things. That's where the power lives. Ignorance is weakness. Knowledge is power. Insights gained from Buddhist practice, especially when integrated with 12-Step principles; give us a kind of spiritual knowledge that goes beyond the mind. Keep that in mind, but don't go out of your mind trying to figure it out. Relax. Be Present. Go deep. Let the wisdom arise. But don't hold on to it! It's also impermanent—subject to change.

Reflections

What is permanent and not subject to change? Explain.

_____

_____

_____

_____

_____

_____

_____

_____

_____

_____

_____

_____

_____

Samsara: Cycle of Change

Samsara: an infinite cycle of infinite sufferings.
It's big. But it's not permanent from my point of
view. Buddhists in particular set a goal for emptying
of samsara of every last suffering being. We're all
born and we all suffer; we have moments of not
suffering so much, relatively speaking, then we
suffer some more. We get sick, we get old (if we're
lucky), then we die. Then our karmic potential, not
our consciousness or identity per se, reincarnates
into another physical body of some kind, or maybe
into a formless realm. There are samsaric cycles
within samsaric cycles within samsaric cycles.

When we look at the whole picture, our entire
situation is called samsara. It's the realm of desire
and suffering. Our potential for suffering is unlim-
ited because causes lead to effects, which lead to
causes, ad-infinitum.

No one can say there is an end to suffering as
long as we have no path to liberate ourselves from
suffering. But in order to enter on a path we need
to have certain capacities. Only humans have the
capacity to think at a level high enough to understand these principles. For that reason, our human
rebirth is said to be precious.

One of the big realizations that help us on the path is the ability to look at life as it is, and let it teach us what the Buddha understood. Life is suffering. Suffering has its causes: attachment, aversion, ignorance. Those causes can be changed to end suffering. Vows are one way to do it. Get on that path, end your suffering, and help others. That's the program. That's the power of vow.

Reflections

Describe your own cycles of change.

_____

_____

_____

_____

_____

_____

_____

Precious Human Rebirth: Use it or Lose it

As humans we have brains that allow us intelligence. We can read, we can study, we can meditate, we can practice. Sometimes we look at animals and think they have it better. But do they? Can they fend for themselves once domesticated; survive in the wild with other predators, especially humans, and other threats to their existence? We can't really see the beings in the other realms of Buddhist cosmology, but besides Animals we can imagine the Hell Beings, Hungry Ghosts, Jealous Gods and Gods. Some say that all of the realms are symbolic or mental. Perhaps, but they're realms of suffering nonetheless. If Hell is a place that "we" go to or if Hell is a state of mind, it ain't fun. Right?

As humans we have opportunity. In the entire spectrum of possibility, it is extremely rare, and astronomically uncommon to be born human and be in a world where a Buddha realizes Buddhahood, the ultimate Awakening. We're even more fortunate to have more than a passing interest in the path of total liberation that Buddhism offers. We are really, really in good shape if we can find a teacher whom we want to follow and a teaching that we can commit to. Bugs don't do it. Fish can't do it.

Monkeys, though they might be smart, are probably more interested in picking fleas off of each other than learning to contemplate impermanence.

These four points; karma, impermanence, samsara, precious human rebirth, are fundamental to Buddhist thought. Without them, we have no path. With them, we can understand something of vows and why we might consider taking them. We've looked at these and the Four Noble Truths. Along the way I've tried to shed light on how these relate to the addict's state of mind.

Reflections

Why is your life precious? What actions can you take to live by that understanding?

_____

_____

_____

_____

_____

_____

_____

_____

_____

Eight Worldly Concerns

Some of the things that we learn to rethink when we're on the Buddhist path are the 'Eight Worldly Concerns.' Prior to entering the Buddhist path, all of one's actions are preoccupied with:

Hope for happiness and fear of suffering
Hope for fame and fear of insignificance
Hope for praise and fear of blame
Hope for gain and fear of loss

I mention these here because as we develop our experiences on the path of recovery and the path to enlightenment, it's important to note when these perspectives begin to shift. These shifts don't happen overnight. If we're addicts we can understand how long it took to go through the stages of change: from not having a problem; to thinking about how we might have a problem; to looking into ways to solve the problem, before finally taking some actions to solve the problem; until it becomes clear that major shifts of this magnitude are a process. They are not usually an event.

Dharma practice; into mindfulness; into spiritual progress are like this. Just like this. I'm not trying to overwhelm everyone with information. Each principle offers many ideas to think about. But I think it's important to lay out the roadmap. It takes much preparation to build an addiction and a ton of work to get clean. If we see the path from a bird's eye view, then we have a better chance to apply our tools when everyday life situations arise. If we can't apply the tools when we need them most, they're of no value. We shouldn't wait until we need them to know about them and we should apply them to everyday life.

> *If we lose the desire to be center stage, we'll know our practice is working.*

When we do practice for a while and notice that our hope for happiness has been replaced with acceptance, then we're making progress. If we lose the desire to be center stage, we'll know our practice is working. When praise is less important than service, we can see how our views have shifted. When we can sit in contemplation with no hope for gain or fear of loss, we might well be on our way to being an enlightened Buddha. The vows give us this opportunity to practice and help us hold the space for ourselves to practice. Progress will happen. Perfection is possible—but only when we positively work toward it!

Reflections

What are the main things that you're concerned about?

_____

_____

_____

_____

_____

What Makes a Vow?

A Vow by Any Other Name

What is a vow, in the secular sense? Most of us have some familiarity, but it may be helpful to get specific. In addition to marriage vows, we vow to tell the truth, the whole truth and nothing but the truth in court. We also make vows and oaths meant to uphold the principles of our professions. But let's be clear about the similarities and differences between types of vows in secular and religious contexts. We'll look at some basic definitions of power and of vows. I've selected those that are most relevant to our discussion. According to dictionary.com:

"Vow

Noun 1. a solemn promise, pledge, or personal commitment: marriage vows; a vow of secrecy.

2. a solemn promise made to a deity or saint committing oneself to an act, service, or condition.

3. a solemn or earnest declaration.

Verb 4. to make a vow of; promise by a

vow, as to God or a saint: to vow a crusade or
a pilgrimage.

5. to pledge or resolve solemnly to do,
make, give, observe. They vowed revenge.

6. to declare solemnly or earnestly; assert
emphatically (often followed by a clause as
object): She vowed that she would take the
matter to court.

7. to dedicate or devote by a vow: to vow
oneself to the service of God."

It's fascinating that a vow can be a noun or a verb.
The verb definitions given for the acts of taking vows
work pretty well in the Buddhist sense. The doing
words make sense because vows are actions. We can
make our vows, take our vows and declare our vows
in front of a teacher and *a sangha: spiritual community*. In my opinion, however, the standard definition
of vow as a noun is not sufficient to understand the
true nature and power of 'vow' in Dharma.

Reflections

What is a vow, in the secular sense?

_____

_____

_____

_____

_____

_____

_____

_____

The noun definition is where things are different. The Buddhist vow is more than a promise. The vow has more conviction because it is based on more knowledge than a promise. Promises are based on feeling something on an emotional level. For example, if I lie and feel guilty I can confess to the person that I lied to and promise not to lie again. Confession has its function as a spiritual tool (we'll explore this in the Purification section later). A promise based on a feeling uses emotional logic. Emotional logic is fuzzy, at best and a total distortion at its worst.

For example, if we take a moment to look within and ask ourselves how we feel. Just check in. Ask yourself, "How am I feeling?" Try to be specific. It's not sufficient to answer as if we ran into a friend at Starbuck's with, "I'm good."

Reflections

Discuss your five most frequent emotions.

_____

_____

_____

_____

_____

_____

_____

_____

Buddhists look within in a more inquisitive, specific way.

What am I feeling? We might notice that we're feeling anxiety.

_____

_____

_____

_____

_____

_____

Where is the feeling? Does it move or is it in just one place? Where is that place? Can you touch it? Maybe we feel peaceful or happy or sexual or depressed.

_____

_____

_____

_____

How is it, this feeling, just now? Can we observe without grasping? Where did the feeling come from? Can we find its beginning? How long has it been there and how long will it last? Does it change?

_____

_____

_____

_____

_____

As we can see from this type of meditation, emotion is not as clear or precise as something like a physical experience. My head hurts. It hurts because I bumped it. We pull a muscle or stub our toe and we can point to it and explain where it is, how it got there and hopefully, when it will go away. This is a bit of a generalization, because if we try to meditate on the feeling of pain we may have a similar dilemma as when we explore the origins, quality and location of emotion. But the point is that physical experience is generally more concrete and clearer than emotional experience.

For this reason, in Buddhist thought, emotion lies at the root of our problems. From a psychological perspective that may seem unhealthy. In a Western sense, we think of blocking our emotions as negative. We need to learn to feel our feelings and not run from them in recovery as well. In the Buddhist approach, at least as I see it, practice doesn't mean that we don't feel our feelings. That would be an incorrect interpretation of the teaching.

What it does mean is that as Buddhist practitioners we work on being 'mind possessors' not 'mind slaves'. In this case, we're not blindly driven by our passions. From the perspective of a renunciate monk who lives by extreme rules, it might make sense to completely block all emotion. But I'm critical of this approach. I feel that it makes sense to open ourselves to what we feel—without reacting to it. That takes guts, honesty and practice. Vows such as those we're about to discuss can support us in this process.

Admittedly, my approach is more *tantric: based on principles of energy,* than it is *sutric: based on principles of renunciation.* In Buddhism we work with *The Three Gates: body, energy and mind.* If we think about the principle of self-control, it's easy to see how we can apply it on all three levels.

From the physical level, we stop any actions, which may cause harm. This is the grossest dimension of our being. It's more solid, easy to see. Emotional energy is subtler and therefore more difficult to spot and control. If we practice on the energy level, we allow ourselves to feel the feeling. But we have to use a lot of self-control to keep the feeling from manifesting in an action. Sex is a good example. Can we control our orgasm to the extent that we can stop or begin it at will at any stage? Some tantric, Taoist, and other practices teach us to do just that.

Self-control is even more difficult to practice on an even more subtle mental level. Can we stop our thoughts? Why would we want do to that? After all, our mind is our own. No one knows what we're thinking? Yet if we understand how karma works, we can see that there is no single effect from any single cause. Every event is the result of infinite causes and is the trigger of infinite results. On this very subtle level, it's quite difficult to notice our thoughts before they become feelings and actions. We have to develop a watchful meditator's eye. It can take a very long time and a lot of diligence. Once we see them as they arise, we're free to choose. Do I want to indulge in this thought? Can I let it go? How much practice do you think this level of skill takes? In Buddhism, we call this meditator's skill *discriminating awareness.*

With or without this awareness, we can prac-

> *Every event is the result of infinite causes and is the trigger of infinite results.*

tice and ultimately develop our ability to act based on compassion, bodhicitta in Sanskrit. There are many practices in the Mayahana, such as Tonglen: exchanging self for others, which aim to cultivate such compassion. It's easy enough to feel compassion for those we love. But the practice of doing the work of the Buddha has many levels. We can try to experience our feelings of love for those closest, to the neutral, faceless crowds and on to our greatest enemies. Remember, we're all connected. Buddhists call this interdependence. But to take that idea from an intellectual to a sophisticated, highly evolved experiential level is some serious skill. See the 12-Step Buddhist or other works such as those by Pema Chodron for more on these Bodhisattva practices. There are also vows that relate to the practices of the bodhisattva: path of compassion. I'll show you a simple way to take that vow in a bit.

There is another main difference between Buddhist vows and those made to a deity, organization or individual. A Buddhist vow isn't made to a God or external authority. Undoubtedly, from certain Buddhist perspectives it can be thought of that way. Some even pray to Buddha. But Buddhist practice moves along a continuum, from saving ourselves to saving other beings to working for the benefit of the whole cosmological enchilada.

Another way to look at the stages of practice is from Outer to Inner to Secret and Most Secret. The theory, practice and application moves from gross to subtle to more subtle layers. That means we could begin with an external prayer to a being perceived as an outside entity—if that's what we need. There's no rule against saying, Dear Buddha, please help me. But in general, most Western practitioners who look to Buddhism are trying to get away from what they perceive to be dogmatic practices. That doesn't mean that in a pinch, we can't squeak out a prayer to the Buddha. He's an enlightened being. Prayer works. Don't hold back if this helps to find an answer. Just remember that the Dharma is a continuum. We can enter the stream wherever we find ourselves. When we practice renunciation, we go against the stream of karma.

Practice moves us to the many levels of our inner life. I mentioned earlier how we can practice with our body, speech, or mind. Another way to practice internally is to receive tantric initiation. When we enter that path, we're trained to develop the understanding of the qualities of an enlightened being. In this system, there are no limits. In tantrism, we go with the stream, not against it. Every experience becomes a possibility for transfomation. We don't avoid experiences as tantric practitioners. Caution: this is advanced practice.

> *Circumstances change and our practice should change to work with our circumstances.*

Depending on the system in which we study, this process can happen sometimes quickly, sometimes slowly, as we say in 12-Step. When we work on the inner level from this tantric perspective, we eventually train to see ourselves as the deity. We develop that and eventually accomplish the wisdom of the deity. Again, be careful not to confuse tantra with some sort of dogmatic authority system. It's very different. As far as I know there are no practices in Christianity where Christians look at themselves as God. Yet in Tantric Buddhism, that is exactly the path. Be aware that there are many versions of this in Hinduism and Buddhism. There also exist a huge variety of traditions and systems in which to practice. They're not all the same.

Ultimately, our practice must move to the space beyond words or concepts of deities and non-deities. We may be attracted to one of these styles of practice and repulsed by others. That may shift back and forth on the path. The important thing is that we start where we are and take one step at a time. Stay fluid. Remember—let go of the inner dogma. Circumstances change and our practice should change to work with our circumstances.

That means we should educate ourselves on more than one system. The more familiar we are with the entire scope of teaching and practice, the more tools we have in our spiritual toolkit. The spiritual handyman always carries the right tool for the job. And we never know in life what kind of troubleshooting we'll be called upon to do. Those of us who vow to save all beings will want to have as many skills as we can gain, seeing as that's a pretty voluminous vow!

It should be said that some people prefer to use one practice forever. I respect that. I personally prefer to have a variety of ways to handle the complex range of situations possible. That's the way I've been taught, so that's what I try to pass on to everyone.

Reflections

_____

_____

_____

_____

_____

Addicts Make Empty Promises

A picture is worth a thousand words. The promises of an addict are worth nothing. Past a certain point in the process of addiction, there's one way to know an addict is lying: if their lips are moving. We've lied to ourselves.

> *A picture is worth a thousand words. The promises of an addict are worth nothing.*

We've lied to those who love us. Nobody believes us anymore. Yet we blame others for our pain. We complain that they don't get us. From the perspective of recovery, one of the principle qualities that we develop is to take responsibility for ourselves. But in pre-recovery, our attitude is on the opposite end of the spectrum. Addicts that are in the disease, (actively using), say the darnedest things:

This is the last time.
Just one won't hurt.
No, I'm just tired.
I'll never drink again.
I have to stop.

This is killing me.
I didn't mean to hurt you, it won't happen again.
I'm just going in for some food.
I'm never going back to that.
I'll quit tomorrow.
The ATM ate my card...Can I borrow $20?
I'm waiting to hear back from a friend. Can I crash here for a little while?
You gonna finish that?

Reflections

How many times have we heard or said stuff like this? Name a few.

_____

_____

_____

_____

Whether it's smoking, food, sex, drugs, or alcohol—addiction always wins—until we learn to surrender. In my experience, we can't win the battle with our addictions until we lay down our best weapons. Denial is the first barrier to break. Recovery is a process that starts when we admit that we need help. But that is only the beginning. The admission itself is not sufficient for long-term recovery, let alone spiritual enlightenment.Most addicts know what it means to make false promises. We know how to get what we want. We just tell people what they want to hear. It doesn't matter if it's the

> *Recovery is a process that starts when we admit that we need help.*

truth. Because of this, we may feel that taking a vow is the same as making another empty promise. It isn't—if we understand what we're doing. I'll show you how to use the muscle that is available when taking vows. In recovery we often call this surrender to win. It's about giving up personal power to gain spiritual power. But it's normally surrender to a "creator God." We'll talk about how Buddhism is different; yet can be used in similar ways. One thing that Buddhism and 12-Step principles have in common is the development of compassion and an attitude of service. Vows take that to a whole new level.

A real vow is not an impulsive, fear based, empty promise. Promises can be sincere. A vow is more serious. It's a spiritual covenant, especially if it's taken in that context, with that understanding, in front of others who have the same understanding. A vow should be, based on a clear view of our situation. That doesn't mean our circumstances are simple. They're usually pretty complicated. There are several causes and several results—too many to imagine. But as we use our meditation practice to consider what our situation actually is—not some fantasy—we begin to sense the essence of life as it is. We can pretend to "be here now" all day long. When we're really present, we feel everything.

Many people use a false sense of spirituality to actually avoid being present. This error is sometimes referred to as spiritual bypassing. It's like we go into a meditation-induced buffer zone to escape our pain, then the Dharma becomes an obstacle. I've spent many hours in meditation trying not to bypass what's really going on. It is an incredibly difficult practice that takes power. Sometimes we have the power, sometimes we don't.

To be really present is a very deep experience. In fact, I think there is no end to it. When we fully realize the infinity of the now we can become Buddhas capable of some miraculous shit. We shouldn't kid ourselves; we should rid ourselves of self, and all of the lies and deceptions, which keep the smoke screen intact. Vow to do that. Vow to see life as it really is. Not just a little, but all the way. Penetrate to the core. We know it can be done. We have the Buddha archetype. We all do. Get the Buddha within us online. That's what vows are all about.

The Buddha laid out the facts of our condition so that we could understand the problem of existence, and the solution to suffering. But the density of our delusion is old—ancient. This makes it tough to see the truth. Use tenacity to see through the delusions. Vows give us that strength. It's more than saying, "I promise to look into getting enlightened some time. Now pass the popcorn." A promise may be based on a feeling of weakness. A vow is based on power. We gain power through confidence. We get confident with experience.

The power of vow is the power of examining whom we are, creating a vision of who we want to be, and deciding how we're going to live. It's up to us. Do you think you can handle that? *...the work is ours to do.* I do. In 12-Step we often say, "God doesn't give us more than we can handle." From the Buddhist perspective, instead of a creator God giving us what he determines that we deserve, Buddha gives us teachings to help us work from where we are. We take the responsibility for our own enlightenment.

We can pray for some help, and we may get it. But the work is ours to do.

It may sound daunting, but if we shift our thinking some, we can see how practice works to our benefit. A shift in view is critical for spiritual growth. Vows ask for a shift in view to begin, and then they help us deepen that 'right view.' Remember that within Buddhist paths the ideas are often very different than what we're used to in our culture. Don't let that difference stand in the way. We start where we are.

Reflections

_____

_____

_____

_____

_____

_____

_____

_____

Love and other Vows

In the West, we consider vows such as marriage vows to be promises that we make with God, our community and our partner. We vow to love, honor and cherish. But those vows are broken so often, it can be disheartening. It might make more sense to vow to be 'Present,' as long as we both shall live.

Rates of divorce give us reason to doubt how well we do when we solemnly swear to have and to hold, till death do us part. But how often do those stick? Our divorce rate in the United States is still about fifty percent. It doesn't take much research to see how easy it is to break marriage vows. Broken vows mean broken homes. Many kids grow up in single parent families, often with siblings from different parents. For them the idea of the sanctity of marriage

> *It might make more sense to vow to be 'Present,' as long as we both shall live.*

may hold less value than children who observe long term, healthy marriages. We just don't grow up with the same expectations on commitment as were prevalent in other eras.

It's true that some people of exceptional character, commitment, or luck are able to keep marriage vows. Maybe it's because they have strong faith, the support of their spiritual community, family, and culture that the marriage vows are upheld.

Sometimes these types of vows can be based on fear. Catholics, for example, may fear recrimination from the church or disharmony in the extended family if they get divorced. Still, some would rather risk going to hell later to get out of hell now. In recovery, many people reject religious concepts such as being sent to hell for acting badly. A recent Facebook post said of [...the difference between the 12-Step spirituality and religion that one], "...is a spiritual, not religious program. Narcotics Anonymous (NA) never opened the gates of heaven to let me in. But NA did open the gates of hell to let me out."

In a Buddhist sense, it's normally quite different. Some traditions use the ideas of hell and the different other realms as motivation to practice. I think that in monasteries the ideas of going to the hell realms for breaking *root: main vows* can be used for control of the monastics. But the essence of the Buddhist teaching is not to terrorize people into getting spiritual.

For addicts, the scare tactics of religion don't work well. Most of us have already lived in the hell of our own traumatic childhoods and subsequent addictions. Fear may sometimes help get us clean and sober, but I doubt that it's of much value in keeping us that way. I did so many things in my addiction that I was afraid to do and that I said I'd never do. Somehow our brains can shut down when we're seeking or using our drugs of choice. The consequences of our actions are blotted out. Our decision-making is impaired.

It's very easy to forget the consequences of addictive behavior. Some brain research suggests that the reward centers of the brain that are responsible to remember the danger of addiction actually malfunction, perhaps due to low levels of dopamine. But we do remember the feeling of being high, possibly because dopamine affects memory when it spikes as it does during a high reward peak. That could add some understanding to the baffling mystery of chronic relapsers. Despite their best intentions and promises, they never seem to attain long-term sobriety. They relapse over and over and over, even when they're seemingly doing very well.

Promises and vows out of fear of punishment normally have a sense of resentment tied to them. There is an element of the unknown. From a monotheistic perspective we may wonder, "How will God punish me this time?" With Buddhist tools we can step on to a path with much more certainty than whatever the will or whim of a creator God may or may not be.

Reflections

What feelings do you have about making vows?

_____

_____

_____

_____

_____

_____

Vows Build Our Practice Muscle

Like physical muscles, our spiritual muscles atrophy when not used. They also get stronger with practice. We need vows because the power of vow makes our practice stronger, and more concrete. We know what we're doing and why we're doing it. The vow helps our brain regulate its activity because when we have the vow in mind it serves as a guide. This is especially useful when doubt creeps into our brain's reward system and forgets the negative impact of thought, emotion, and behavior. These obstacles will occur for everyone. The obstacles are actually the reason that the vows work the way they do. Sometimes we might think, "Oh no, I could never keep that vow. Maybe someday when I have stronger will-power." But the vows are meant for those of us who know will-power is not enough. It is precisely because we need the support of the vow to aid our will that we take the vows. If we were perfect, why would we need vows? In this sense, the obstacle becomes the opportunity for practice.

...the vows are meant for those of us who know will-power is not enough.

The principal obstacle to practice seems to be that we generally lack discipline. This is exactly the quality that we need to develop. The vow helps put discipline in perspective. Lack of discipline is a pretty common problem among practitioners. In my experience, it's also the plague of people in recovery. Vajrapani Institute did a survey asking about obstacles that people encounter in their spiritual practice. Here are some interesting results:

Top difficulties included:

"Lack of willpower/discipline" (48% of all respondents)
"It's hard to keep a regular practice" (47%)
"Hard to stay motivated without spiritual community" (30%)
"Lifestyle gets in the way" (24%)

In addition, respondents reported that they needed help with:

A regular meditation practice.
Inspiration to keep them going.
Structure, so they felt like they knew what to do.
A sense of community.

We can take our vows alone, with a friend, in front of a group of monks, or within our own spiritual community. I'll show you how to create the willpower and inspiration. For a sense of community and connectedness, we can find several Buddhist groups in most metro areas, but many parts of the country have fewer options to offer. An alternative, besides moving, would be to join 12-Step Buddhist and other online communities on Facebook, Google Plus and Twitter.

When we talk about taking vows in a Buddhist context, we're using the power of our intention, the power of lineage, the blessings of infinite Buddhas and our sangha near and far. When taken seriously and understood, the principle of vow is one of the most powerful spiritual practices there is. I'll show you some ways to make the power of vow work for you. To get there, we'll use some unconventional tools.

In the process of dealing with vows, we may run into some inner resistance. It's easy to fall into low self-esteem if we don't live up to the high expectations that others or we place on us. On one hand, our expectations may be too low or unrealistic. We need to find the middle ground. In 12-Step, we're used to the thinking that it's progress, not perfection. In spiritual teachings such as Buddhism, we're asked to consider developing the qualities of enlightened beings. This can seem daunting. But we can enter the path right where we stand. We practice where we are. I wrote about this in *Perfect Practice* (amazon.com), where I provided some methods for practicing the *paramitas: perfections of generosity, ethical discipline, patience, diligence, concentration, and wisdom*. We will work on developing these qualities over time.

It's important to understand that spiritual growth doesn't look the same for everyone. It happens on different dimensions at different rates. Ken Wilber's work on the psychograph explains various aspects of ourselves, which develop at different rates throughout the life cycle. It's important to understand that we may be quite evolved in one area such as patience, but very shaky in ethical discipline. If we fall into black and white thinking, we may feel that because we're not skillful in one dimension, we're not doing well. Worse, we may feel that we don't deserve the good things that recovery and spirituality have to offer, which may lead to relapse. It's important that we don't let our weaknesses shame us out of knowing our strengths. With the achievement of meditative stabilization, which is made possible by keeping vows, we can learn to be present with the good and the bad, the strong and the weak, the suffering and the bliss in our own hearts and in the mind streams of other beings.

One way to see these parts of ourselves is to look at our archetypes, which I called 'Aspects of Self' in *The 12-Step Buddhist*. These aspects are energy templates, through which our life energy is expressed. They can take many forms and are often in opposition to each other. When one aspect is relegated to the background, it becomes a shadow archetype. The shadow aspect leaks out in often-unexpected ways. This is especially important work in terms of our relationship to power. Let's talk about power as it relates to vows.

Power and the Vow

Dictionary.com: Power-
Noun:
ability to do or act; capability of doing or
accomplishing something.
Verb:
to inspire; spur; sustain: A strong faith in
divine goodness powers his life.

Reflections

What are your feelings when you think about
power, and powerlessness?

_____

_____

_____

_____

_____

_____

_____

_____

Although our first step of twelve asks us to admit powerlessness, we do still have the ability to act. We admit that we can't control our addiction. But it's not as if we literally can't still achieve important goals. In recovery people often act as if they have lost all sense of personal power. It just isn't true. The admission of powerlessness is about giving up the fantasy that we're more powerful than our addictions. Later in the steps, we can learn to surrender our ego drives to higher purposes. But that's not the way some people seem to think in recovery. There is a tendency to equate this initial sense of powerlessness with a variant of learned helplessness: like a dog that's been beat too much.

We might claim powerlessness as an excuse for our behavior or situations. But we do have the ability

We might claim powerlessness as an excuse for our behavior or situations.

to make informed choices. When we enter into the sacred power of vow, we can and will fail at keeping our vows. Bad karma will be created. But there are practices to correct that too. No one keeps his or her vows perfectly. Don't think of taking vows as a setup for failure. We always have the capability of retaking the vows, thus reaffirming our commitment. In fact, it's common for practitioners to retake their vows three or more times per day. The verb definition of vow as action comes into play as we find inspiration and motivation to sustain these commitments.

The issue some of us may have with taking a vow is that we think it means giving up some or all of our power. Power over what: control, choice, and the direction of our lives. But the power of taking a vow lies in its sacred nature. The vow gives us power—

it's not the other way around. Because we accumulate merit in the sanctity of the vow, it affects our circumstances. The more we keep our vows, the more merit we collect and the better our situation becomes. We're tempted less. It might be easy to confuse this with the notion that if we behave, Santa Claus gives us a present, or that God is watching us. In Buddhism, that is not how it's explained. We own our karma. Every moment. This is what taking responsibility means. We should know what we're getting into when we take vows.

When we keep our vows, we accumulate merit. Conversely, when we break them, the backlash is more serious than it would be without the vow. Powerful karmic seeds are sown with the vows, combined with our awareness through meditation and study—not just books but the ongoing study of our own mind. Our intention and action and satisfaction all sow karmic seeds. When we keep the vow, we're protected by the vow. We can enjoy sweetness. When we break the vow, we get served that rotten fruit as the result. This kind of thinking may take a little getting used to. As always, try it out. We must look at our step work or a chronicle of our life to understand how the causes led to effects. It's not always so simple, however, to trace the causes of events. Many seeds are sown in infinite lives. The seeds only ripen when the secondary causes appear. No sunshine, nutrients, and water means no tree. That means no fruit.

In recovery, we have a form of a vow as part of some of the steps. In the 3rd of the 12 Steps, we make a decision to turn our will and our lives over to the care of God, as we understand God. This may seem like a failure at first, but actually gives us more power than we could gain by the unaided will alone:

"And how shall he ever straighten out that awful jam that cost him the affection of his family and separated him from them? His lone courage and unaided will cannot do it. Surely he must now depend on Somebody or Something else." -AA Twelve Steps and Twelve Traditions

Another way of looking at the issue of power from the 12-Step perspective is, "Surrender to win." The typical, creator God application would mean that we give up, and then God gives us what we need. From a non-spiritual point of view, we transfer our power from a weak spot in our ego to a stronger place from within ourselves. If I give up hate and find love instead I have surrendered to win. From a spiritualist perspective, maybe we've forgotten our own divine nature. But that doesn't mean that the spiritual warrior within has left us. We just have to access that source. We do that by "turning it over" to a power greater than our limited sense of self, or our emotions, or our standard habits. What do we turn over? The vows are our guidelines. We turn our power of choice over. If we have an automatic response or an emotion based reaction then we can learn, with practice, to consider turning it over to the power of the vow. The vows then, become our higher power. No creator God needed. The buck starts and ends with us.

The power that we need may seem to be outside of us, but it's not. In order to learn this, we surrender our self-will. That requires a transfer of power from the unaided will to a will that is able to turn to a different aspect of self for strength. Simply put, we just have to stop acting out of patterns based on trauma, bad reasoning and short-term memory. In principle it's the same process as turning it over to God. We just have to re-think it a little to understand this as 12-Step Buddhists or any other secular or spiritual perspective.

Again, this filtering to make the 12 Steps work for us doesn't mean that we need a new program or that we argue these points with other people. If we're evolved, we can apply this knowledge within ourselves with no need to prove anything or start any revolutions. The only revolution that needs to happen is the one on the inside. I call this the involution.

> *The only revolution that needs to happen is the one on the inside.*

And now for some bad news. The patterns of addiction don't leave us just because we get clean. I proved this to myself when I relapsed after a decade of sobriety. The old mental designs normally stay dim while we're active in recovery. When we give them juice in the form of our intention, action and satisfaction, they light up like a power station. The principle of vows is that we increase our good actions while we reduce the negative. I don't think that we can somehow erase the patterns, thus becoming non-addicts, until we achieve the total realization of Buddhahood. At that point our addiction to self-cherishing disappears. Then we transcend paths. In the meantime, we're on the path and working to develop.

Reflections

If you're an addict in recovery, how have your addicted patterns continued even though you're clean?

_____

_____

_____

_____

_____

_____

We must always be careful about how developed we think we are. There are way too many people out there who think they're enlightened just because they've had an enlightening moment here and there. These experiences can be profound, of course. They can motivate and inspire us to do great things. But the full enlightenment experience is the absolute dissolution of self. It includes the ability to transcend space, time and physical limitations, like bodies. Those who have experienced _siddhis: powers obtained are the ability to manifest in any form, clairvoyance, and omniscience,_ understand this transcension. When we experience moments of clarity it is fantastic. But keep it real. Stay humble. Keep working.

And now for the good news: we can make new patterns! The new ones won't erase the old tunes that play endlessly in our heads. But we can learn to sing new songs, for sure. In 12-Step, we hear a lot about not listening to "old tapes." We learn through recovery tools to play different sounds, speak new words (right speech) to others and ourselves. Some

of us are old enough to remember when we played
out our cassettes of Billy Idol's *Rebel Yell* or Michael
Jackson's *Thriller*. Cassette tapes are made from bits
of metal glued to plastic tape. As the metal wears
off, the quality of the audio is drastically reduced.
When we wear out our favorite tune, whether it's
Billy Jean or *I Don't Deserve a Good Relationship*, the
sound quality fades over time. Yet we keep listening,
as if it were a brand new track. With the Third Step,
turning over our power of choice, and the vows, we
change the channel to a more powerful, clear transmission of digital quality sound.

The transfer of power from self-will to the choice
the vow makes for us is really a transformation of
our relationship to power. Many addicts feel a strong
fear response when they are confronted with power.
For a lot of us, our experience with those who've
had authority over us has been traumatic, even
brutal. Our ideas of external power are transferred
from influential figures such as police, parents, and
teachers. When we have abuse histories, our relationship to power is likely to be one of retreat or
retaliation. Often there is no space in our minds and
bodies to learn new ways to relate. Spiritual vows
can help us create that space.

Next we'll consider the Voice Dialogues to make
some room in our hearts. These can be approached
in a variety of ways, as I wrote about in *The 12-Step
Buddhist*. When we deal with a voice, the most
important skill to learn is to simply notice it. There's
a lot of power in mindful awareness of an aspect
of self. We can meditate on it, read aloud with the
suggested dialogue, or go off on our own dialogue. It
works best verbally, but a written or mental practice
can also be effective. We can create art; paint, draw,
play guitar from an aspect of self. Try it out. Let the

Voice of Fear, or another voice, do some coloring. The voices aren't always able to express with language. Consider that some of these are deeply buried in the psyche. For some aspects, individual or group therapy may be the best option. For people with serious mental health issues, please seek professional advice.

Reflections

_____

_____

_____

_____

_____

_____

How to **5** Vow?

"Depending on the number of precepts one promises to follow, there are four types of lay practitioners: a lay practitioner who observes one precept alone (to abstain from murder); one who observes some precepts (to abstain also from stealing); one who observes most of the precepts (to abstain also from untruths); and the perfect lay practitioner who follows all five precepts, including forsaking adultery and drinking alcohol." –Jamgon Kongtrul

We'll approach the practice of vows (precepts) from a variety of angles. These should offer unique perspective and insight. One method we'll use concerns our inner voices. In *The 12-Step Buddhist*, in our retreats and workshops and in *Perfect Practice* we work with what I call 'Aspects of Self.' They're also called archetypes. Knowing about them is a very potent tool. There are different ways to learn about the aspects. The method that I use involves stepping outside of our "self" and speaking as a particular voice in the first person. So if we speak as the Voice of Anger, we'd speak as if Anger were a separate person, within the whole person.

But words are only one expression of voice. I think of voice as energy, which can be expressed verbally, non-verbally, in dreams, in art, dance, yoga, and relationships. Speaking is a very powerful way to get familiar with our inner aspects. This 'Aspects of Self' method was originally written about in the book *Embracing Ourselves: The Voice of Dialogue Manual* by Hal and Sidra Stone.

It gives a voice to parts of us that may not feel empowered or that may feel entitled. Here's how it works.

The Vows and the Voices

The concept of speaking in voices is simple yet profound. We've all had moments where we didn't feel ourselves. In a burst of anger we say things we don't mean, perhaps to our loved ones, in a voice that sounds a bit too much like one of our parents or other critics. Just before a significant move forward in life, maybe a career change, we're overcome with doubt and dread. We meet the kind of person we've been waiting for only to sabotage the relationship. Sometimes there's a clear voice in our head driving us, other times just a feeling. We learn to adapt, overcome and move beyond our limitations on some fronts, but maybe not all of them.

These setbacks, based on habitual patterns hard wired into our brains from genetics, trauma, and learning can happen despite our progress in other areas. If we have all or nothing, black and white thinking, which is quite common among addicts but certainly not limited to that group, we may be confused. How can we do great on one level and terrible on another—at the same time? It's easier to understand if we consider that we exist on many dimensions simultaneously.

In the psychograph, we exist and develop different talents, capacities, and skills, according to Ken Wilber. Body, mind, sprit, soul, evolve along cognitive, moral, interpersonal, spiritual and affective lines. He calls these aspects waves or, "strong currents in the River of Life." Wilber also says,

> "A person can be highly evolved in some lines, medium in others and low in still others, but that overall development follows no linear sequence whatever."

This is important information for anyone, especially addicts. We have a tendency to give in to black and white thinking. We feel that we're either better than others or sadly inferior. It's very difficult to accept ourselves as awesome at some things and not so good in other ways. Non-addicts can learn from our condition because we all have a tendency to polarize our thinking about others and ourselves. In addicts, it's somewhat exaggerated. The vows can help us gauge our progress on some of these dimensions, particularly if we track our actions. A fellow yoga teacher friend keeps a goal chart on his wall. Each day when he wakes up, he sets some goals for what he's going to eat, how he'll exercise and so on. Then at the end of the day he gives himself stars for a job well done. What if we did something like this for our vows or other spiritual practices? Meditation gets a star. Yoga gets two stars. A green smoothie: three stars! Did we act out in anger, engage in sexual misconduct, or forget to take refuge? Better put an ugly black X!

We could even track something like this in teams, with our 12-Step sponsors in a shared Google document on our phones. The technology is there. And some brain research supports the practices of working in groups to change behaviors. For example, runners who run in groups scored higher on word memorization. People in 12-Step communities stay sober together. Those in sanghas can also progress together.

The Three Gates: Body, Energy, Mind

We simultaneously live in a physical body, and operate in an energy field, and on a mental plane. These are known as 'The Three Gates.' It's easy to understand when we consider the following: if we were sick, on our dying bed in the hospital and the doctor came in and offered us a new body, most of the time we'd accept. So we know we are not just our physical body. When we run out of steam, we look for ways to get more with a coffee and other stimulants, food, rest, and excitement. If we were losing our minds, in five point restraints, face down on a gurney, and the psychiatrist came up and said, "We can inject a nanobot: tiny microcomputer (See *The Singularity is Near* by Ray Kurzweil) right now and replace your broken mind with a fresh one," we might likely say yes to that. His Holiness Dalai Lama discusses this idea in *The Middle Way: Faith Grounded in Reason* with Geshe Thupten Jinpa.

We exist at the same moment in all of these, but our awareness is normally limited to one at a time. We might at one point feel physically fine but emotionally ill. There are so many dimensions within the levels of body, energy and mind, but the point is clear that we aren't aware of all of them, nor can we develop everything at the same rate and on the same levels. Our meditation can help us get in touch with these parts of ourselves. Many of these ways of being in the world can be explained by the concept of archetypes. I use the terms aspect, archetype and voice interchangeably.

Archetypes: energy patterns are what the medical intuitive Carolyn Myss calls templates, through which our energy is projected. The simple act of being aware of these aspects gives us power. Instead of being blindly driven, we awaken to the desires, motivations, habits, benefits, drawbacks and skills of an individual aspect, as if it were another person. It's not another person; it's a part of us. But to make the mental and energetic shift into awareness, we can use the first person voice. *Shadow aspects: when we're unaware of a part of us, or have pushed it aside, judged or disowned it.* The term shadow doesn't always mean something negative. These are parts of us that aren't out in broad daylight. We can become familiar with these, which helps us become integrated and feel whole, rather than conflicted and fragmented.

If we deny part of ourselves, that part can still influence our feelings, thoughts, and decisions indirectly. Shadow work in psychology is when we deal with unpleasant, disowned, rejected and disconnected part of ourselves. In the Aspects of Self Dialogues, we speak in the first person as the voice of that particular archetype. This allows that aspect to communicate with the rest of us, thus relieving pressure. It doesn't mean that we let a negative side of us take us over. In fact, it works opposite to that. If we don't acknowledge the shadow aspects, they may have subversive power in that they leak, or speak to us in unhealthy ways, because we've denied them.

Reflections

What are some of your shadow aspects?

_____

_____

_____

_____

_____

_____

_____

_____

_____

When I was sober the first time, I tried to lock my Addict in the basement of my mind. It didn't work.

When I put my Addict away as a sober graduate student in psychology, it wouldn't stay put. I've told this story elsewhere so I won't go into much detail. When I stuffed my Addict away in shame, this energy pattern that dominated my life for so long bit me in the ass—hard. I've still got the scars to prove it. I wound up drunk, broke, and alone.

There are many, perhaps thousands of archetypes in the human realm. We may not experience them all, but we have connections to every one of them. Some are main patterns. Common ones that we may have heard about are Victim, Child, Prostitute, Saboteur, Addict, Artist, and Athlete. We'll deal with some that are relevant to addiction, recovery, and Buddhist practice as they pertain to vows.

Some of the voices in our heads will be anti-vow. In other words, they will work to undermine our efforts at spiritual progress. They have this effect when the energy of the aspect isn't integrated into the whole being. A lost child would make up stories without all of the information about his situation. A part of our self, a *soul fragment* as we call it in shamanism, may be completely confused. Pieces of our souls break off from the whole during traumatic experiences. We can see that if we acknowledge a part like this, give it a voice, or a coloring book, it has the opportunity to heal. We can bring our pieces home, as adult, mature versions that are willing and able to collaborate with the whole.

What if our archetype isn't able to deal with a vow? What can we do? What we need to know is that the vow will help our energy go where it needs to go and do what it needs to do. Buddhas can't make us enlightened. But there is medicine available. We can receive help along the path. If we get angry, without the vow we may act on the anger. If we've worked the Fourth Step (taking personal inventory and uncovering our resentments), we may have some insight into our patterns anger, but we most likely won't become miraculously free of anger. Over time, the anger can subside, come up less often and less intensely. If we practice yoga, we can try to take our Voice of Anger into our yoga practice to work with that energy. As we move through our poses, we might listen to the feelings we have from the perspective of this voice. We might feel some tension, and then exhale deeply to let it go. While we learn to release on a muscular level, we train our minds to let go on the emotional level as well.

In the general thinking of recovery, when we learn why we get angry, we realize that nurturing resentments is contrary to our recovery. That's supposed to help us control our behavior. But if we can't restrain ourselves, for whatever reason, we might feel like we're not working on our recovery program. The voices can be powerful and can cause us to feel that we're not growing. Again, it's that tunnel vision from the point of view of the voice. After all, old attitudes, behaviors, and overwhelming emotions can lead to a *slip: relapse.*

For some of us this holding back is pretty difficult. If we have trauma from childhood, were raised in an abusive or otherwise chaotic family, we might not be so good at controlling our anger. It could be beyond our control because the experience of anger takes place on a neurological level, deep in the brain. The response to trauma is a shock. It's automatic and quicker than our reflexes. The response in the brain happens faster than thought. Triggers in the brains of addicts have been measured at 1/8th of a second. The response to a trigger is normally to reach for the drug of choice.

Anger responses can work in the same way. We really need to retrain our brains to respond in healthy ways to all kinds of triggers. Buddhist meditations and vows can help. In fact, there are many sets of practices in Buddhism that are considered 'mind trainings.' It's all mind training, or retraining, in my opinion.

> *...nurturing resentments is contrary to our recovery.*

I've personally spent years in different kinds of therapies working out my childhood anger. It wasn't until I integrated 12-Step work and therapy with Buddhist vows that I was able to make noticeable progress. The ownership of voices such as anger can be extremely powerful in the healing process. But it takes some courage to own up to them.

We may not be aware that we have these different aspects and they can often operate as if they're separate voices in our heads. If we do some work with this, we can learn to spot check the voices that get us into trouble, before it's too late. Then we won't be fooled if one voice is louder than the rest. For example, the Victim archetype sees the world as an aggressor. It doesn't take responsibility. The voice of the Addict sometimes relies on the role of the Victim. When we blame others for our addiction or other problems, we're in Victim mode on some level. The 12 Steps can help us pull out of the blame mode to a degree. Buddhist principles, particularly vows, can take the sense of personal responsibility to a new level.

> *The ownership of voices such as anger can be extremely powerful in the healing process.*

It's to our own advantage that we invite all of our aspects to sit at our table. If we're divided against ourselves we'll stay in a state of tension. It's like family. Without a recovery program, we often operate out of instinct and old patterns. Some may be dysfunctional. Anyone who has experienced their first sober Thanksgiving can attest to this! But if we're practicing recovery and good communication skills while sitting at the dinner table, things go more smoothly. Even our disowned siblings get respect. Buddhist teacher James Low says that we should find ways to collaborate with ourselves. We do this by listening to all aspects. Invite everybody home.

Reflections

What aspects of yourself do you resist inviting home?

_____

_____

_____

_____

The fear of doing this might be that if we allow a negative voice to speak, it may take over. If we have serious mental health issues, then it would probably be best to explore the more intense voices with a willing professional therapist. But in general, the opposite is true. Instead of taking us over, if we listen to a repressed voice it lets off some pressure. We become more relaxed. From a place of relaxed awareness we can make better decisions.

It's important to know that we need to find ways to balance. We can equalize the energy between different aspects so that when the inevitable conflicts of interest arise, we're prepared. It's not so much that the Addict will disappear and become best friends with the Healer. But we can come to an understanding that the Addict is on the same continuum as the Healer. The Addict just uses unhealthy methods to heal deep pain. In that sense the Addict might morph into the Wounded Healer. Many people new to sobriety decide to become treatment counselors for example. When we do some work with aspects such as these we stand a chance of coming to terms with how to live with our own wounds. Then we're better equipped to help others deal with their suffering.

Another skill that we can work on is balance between our whole self and our different parts. We need to learn not to be reactive, and to be more patient with the different energy patterns that make up the whole of who we are. In this sense, meditation is a powerful skill, when used with awareness and intention regarding our aspects. With meditation we learn to quiet the mind, and become able to respond with compassion to "situations which used to baffle us," as we say in 12-Step. From the calm state, we can make choices, rather than over reacting based on our passions.

To achieve the calm state of mind from a recovery perspective, we work on cleaning house, putting our lives in order, righting our broken relationships and adopting an attitude of love and service. Getting right with God, the world and ourselves calms our agitation. This is why in the 12th Step we're said to have had a spiritual awakening. By the time we do all of that work, we've shifted our consciousness, at least temporarily.

In my experience, however, the feeling

> *From the calm state, we can make choices, rather than over reacting based on our passions.*

of serenity wasn't so easy to achieve with the 12 Steps alone. It happened to a degree, but it didn't last long. Our experiences may be different. But what I've noticed is that after doing the 12 Steps for the first time, the sense of stability was impermanent. We say, "This too shall pass." But in Buddhism, the goal is total liberation. We're trained to see that the state of permanent enlightenment is not only possible; it is the goal and the responsibility of those on the path. This is not normal talk in recovery meetings where the older are not always the wiser and the new are not always the least informed.

There is normally quite a range of experience and capacity in the rooms. To me, it's often interesting to hear people with a couple of years sober pros-elytize about how simple it is to work a program. But when we get into later years, or The Funnel, from five to eight or thereabouts, we start to see things in a different light. Does it get better with time? Not always. Some old timers have relapsed or committed suicide. Why? It's not so easy for all of us to maintain the spiritual glow of early sobriety. In fact, with the 12-Step approach alone, I've found it to be impossible. Others may disagree.

From the basic level Buddhist view, the calm state begins with restraint of our passions. We learn to focus the mind in a single pointed way. We turn away from negative feelings before they gain enough power over us to cause harmful behaviors. We prac-tice calming down our lifestyles, restraining our emotions and directing our minds to an object of meditation. This is called a *sutra: the view or the path of renunciation*. Some people feel that this is the only Buddhist practice. That is not correct. To create the calm state is the beginning of Buddhist practice. At some point, we must learn to integrate our deep 'Presence' with movements of thought, energy and form. After all, the universe is moving. Everything moves in the essence-less vast expanse of emptiness, like basic space. We can learn to experience this through different methods. But it's usually pretty hard to get to that stage until we spend some time practicing restraint and learning what it feels like to be in the calm state.

One way to facilitate the calm state is to work with the energies of the mind. The voice dialogues are a way to do just that. To get into the state of mind of a particular voice, spend a few minutes in silent meditation. That will help center the mind. During meditation, consider the topic at hand. Increased mindfulness increases clarity. It's important to move to a deeper level of awareness because we need to make a shift from our normal operating procedure to one that's more contemplative. To change our thinking, we need to see our thinking. To view it clearly takes a long time and a lot of practice for most of us. But we can make a strong beginning with our intention, action, and satisfaction. That's the power of karma, and the power of vow.

The power of vow is not really about losing something. The power of vow is about gaining responsibility. I vow to take my life into my own hands. My choice is to manage desires, intentions, satisfactions, and actions. In a Christian sense, this might mean we pray and wait for a sign from God. But in Buddhist terms, we are responsible. That's not to say that we can't still pray or that we're never going to get a sign. The laws of the universe still function. Enlightened beings can and will help if we ask. But maybe as Buddhists we're a little less superstitious and more pragmatic about the process of receiving wisdom.

Increased mindfulness increases clarity.

Taking and retaking vows as a spiritual practice is like spiritual Vitamin C. It boosts our karmic immune system and protects us from getting spiritually sick—if our behavior matches our vows. When we act against our ethics in general and our sacred vows in particular, it causes a disruption to our energy. That can cause us to feel or fall ill or even draw provocative circumstances to ourselves. That's not healthy. There are many practices that we can do from tantric, yogic, Ayurveda, Taoist, Chinese, Tibetan medicine, and many other traditions.

But our health is our energy and our energy relates to our emotions, which are connected to our behavior. While we're free to do any practices in any tradition, it's probably best to start by taking the responsibility of our wellbeing into our intentions, actions and satisfactions. If we live this way, we do ourselves a lot of good by creating physical, emotional and mental stability.

Again, when we take a vow, we're not asking someone else what to do. This is big people stuff. It takes guts for some of us to feel that we can make good decisions. As we consider vows, we can also use good counsel; sponsors, therapists, and our management teams. When we learn to trust our own principles and our advisors, we can internalize the wisdom and gain the ability to act on our own innate smartness instead of our fear-based programming.

We can say we're surrendering our will: our impulsive, grasping mind, our desire and attachment to ignorance. We turn over our selfish choices to the power of vow, not someone who tells us what to do. No one can make us take a vow, or make us keep or break a vow. The taking of a vow is the taking on of our own deeper power. This act transforms our relationship to power to bring it from outside of us to inside of us.

The taking of a vow is the taking on of our own deeper power.

From my perspective, once taken, a vow cannot be fully recanted. Even if we say it, try to do it, go against it; the sacred covenant cannot be broken. We'd do best to understand this before going forward. To try to separate us from our vows would be like trying to separate our flesh from our bones. My 12-Step sponsor told me this about Step Three, where we make a decision to turn over our will and our lives to a higher power. He said that the only way to take it back is to find someone who both understands what we're doing and approves of it. We'd have to get that person to willingly help us reverse our Third Step, out loud. Monk vows are similar. They have to be taken with a minimum of two monks who keep pure vows and know that the monk-to-be has a pure heart. I think taking the monk vows back would be just as hard as what my sponsor told me about the Third Step, if not harder.

In the ancient monastic texts, it's said that we cannot release our vows unless we have a radical change of view, a sex change or death. I really don't know how they did a sex change in those times, but this is what the texts refer to. Even then, we're karmically bound. What we lose when we release our vows is the protection. As I mentioned at the beginning, we hold a karmic debt and it will be paid. Immeasurable purification would be called for in a situation where we actually gave back our vows this way. Many monks and nuns have given up their vows. His Holiness the Dalai Lama has said, however, that monastics that are naughty would be better off selling sweaters than being in robes. Among those who've given up their vows are poor people whose families sent them to the monasteries for their education. There might be less bad karma in that case. But I've also heard that many who've given up their monastic vows have suffered because of it.

Everything can be purified. But as my teacher says, we need to be careful. Don't create problems. Be present. Do our best. If we commit a *Root Downfall: serious transgression*, it might be hard for us to stay safe long enough to purify. There is an inherent danger in knowing that karma can be purified. Addicts especially might think, "Well I can get away with breaking this vow just this once. I can always purify later."

What I'm going to say next is more of a view from tantra. We should be careful not to use the view to justify the behavior. In other words, if we think that any negative action can be purified, that is a very bad reason to do that negative action. It's like a perversion of the teachings. In NA they call this, "getting over." We know when we're doing it. We cannot play games like this with our spiritual development. The cost will be well out of proportion to the act. We can't "get over", con in the Dharma! The voices that lead us astray can be very subtle. Attachment and addiction can be cunning, baffling and powerful. If our intention is to try to use the Dharma to sidestep the Dharma, we make trouble that will not be easy to repair.

On one hand we should do our best to keep our integrity. We gain self-knowledge in our fourth step inventory process, meditation and through vows. We must be diligent in using what we learn to continually better ourselves. We're going to mess up. It's pretty hard to say we're going to keep our vows perfectly. But we try. When we make mistakes, we also do our best to know what our mistakes were and understand how to do better next time. And we purify constantly. After all, karma is infinite. We live in samsara with infinite sufferings. All of it is the result of karma.

I think it's better to know what we're doing ahead of time, take it very seriously and know what our commitment is. In a way, there's no self to have a vow and no vow to take. But living in that aware-ness moment by moment is a very high level of yogic attainment. We may come in and out of such moments for various lengths of time. But we should be honest about where we really are and what our capacity is. Having a teacher to check in with is pretty important, if not crucial. I'm not sure your 12-Step sponsor would be qualified to help with vows, but maybe they are. I always advocate a management team approach. That's where we gather a small group of people who have our best interest at heart, and are qualified to help us make important decisions. It's pretty hard to get a group of sane, objective people to co-sign a crazy idea.

The power of vow lies in becoming non-dual with our vows. We are living in dualistic vision: our ego against the universe. I feel that the vows such as Refuge Vows will protect us in this life. When we enter the *Bardo: transition stage of Death* (See the *Tibetan Book of the Dead* for an explanation of the *bardos*), the power of vow will bring us back on our next rebirth to a realm where there has been a Buddha, where teachings and a spiritual commu-nity exist. Then, as my teacher says, there is no problem. We continue on the path.

Practice Session with Dialogues

Following is an example of how to practice voice dialogues. There are many ways. As always, with any of the practices that I describe, feel free to practice parts of them separately. For example, opt to just sit silently, or do only the breathing practice. I've incorporated a breath practice here. I've found that breath work is the best way to calm my mind. To learn breath work, I recommend that you take hatha yoga classes that incorporate breathing. *Pranayama: controlled breath* teaches us to breathe on a deep level. But remember, the purpose of yoga is to learn meditation. In fact, the more I do yoga, the more I need the quiet meditation practice. Yoga stirs up immense energy so the breath work and silent sitting are very good ways to balance that. For those of us who already have a yoga practice, the Buddhist meditations will work well with that.

> *... breath work is the best way to calm my mind.*

The general formula for our simple practice session is:

- Set Intention
- Breathe
- Sit
- Meditate
- Dialogue
- Dedicate

Set Intention

Think about what you want to gain from your practice. Why are you doing it? Perhaps it's for some clarity or calmness or to work on a specific problem. It may be helpful to write down your intention. Remember, **intention fuels the accumulation of karma**. Make it count.

What is your intention?

_____

_____

_____

What will you gain from your practice?

_____

_____

_____

Why are you doing it?

_____

_____

_____

Breathe

We'll use a yogic breath practice. Begin with a slow, long inhale. Take the breath in as far as you can, then gently exhale. Add a little more breath to the next inhale. Fill the body with breath from the lower abdomen, to the heart, up into the throat. Hold a moment gently before exhaling slowly. Keep breathing deeply, long, and slow, from the bottom to the center to the top. Hold a little at the top. On the next exhale let all the air out from the top of the body down. This time draw the belly in to the spine. At the end of the exhale pause before breathing in. You can add the victory breath here, which is just a very slight constriction at the back of the throat. Keep these breathing practices going for one to two minutes. Technically you could do this practice for as long as you want. But to begin, just a minute or two is sufficient. It's useful to return to this controlled breathing if you lose focus in meditation. A short breathing session any time during your day helps you to get focused. I wouldn't recommend doing it while operating heavy machinery or performing brain surgery. But before and after are good.

Reflections on your breathing practice:

_____

_____

_____

_____

_____

_____

Sitting Position

Sit in your favorite mediation position for 5-25 minutes. Your back should be straight. Your feet can be on the floor if you want to be seated. Otherwise, you can sit cross-legged, in half-lotus, or on a Japanese meditation bench. The straight back is the important part.

After finding your position and working with your breathing, sit silently and motionless for several minutes. I suggest 15 minutes, but work with the time you have available. Try to limit it to less than 25 minutes. If counting your breath or some other form of focused meditation is part of your regular practice, by all means do that. Otherwise, just be silent and still and present to the experience of silence and stillness. Try to relax, but remain alert. Once you're sitting practice period is complete, then you are ready to begin work with an archetype. Note: below we're using one particular aspect, but this type of session can work with any aspect. Try to focus on one at a time. That said, if it's clear that you're working with the wrong voice for the session, modify it. Try another trait. But it's important to get into a focused, first person account with one aspect at a time. Otherwise, if we work with too many voices we become confused.

Reflections on your "sitting position"

Explain which position you chose:

_____

_____

_____

Why is it comfortable?

_____

_____

_____

How long did you hold your position?

_____

_____

_____

Did you have trouble staying silent and still? If so, reflect on why:

_____

_____

_____

Dialogue

Speak in the first person as the voice that represents Fear of Power. One option is to follow along with the example below. Another is to write your own first person statement as this voice. You might work with a teacher, counselor, spiritual guide or good friend on this.

The general questions to ask the voice you're working with may be:

Who are you? (Name your Aspect:)

_____

_____

_____

What is your job? (All aspects have a function, Identify it:)

_____

_____

_____

From your point of view, what is the world all about? (This is the point of view of this aspect.)

_____

_____

_____

How do you help the self? (All aspects have some merit.)

_____

_____

_____

What happens when you go too far? (Conversely, aspects can have too much influence.)

_____

_____

_____

How do you harm the self?

_____

_____

_____

What do you need the self, the whole self, to know?

_____

_____

_____

The wisdom in the practice is in the understanding of both the negative and the positive effects of an aspect. Note that the aspect speaks about the self as if the self were someone else, and vice versa.

What do you need the self to know? This is critical. Let the voice say what it needs the whole self or the rest of the selves to know.

If you have someone to help you with your Voices, have them ask the questions. This is the important part: answer as that particular Voice. That's how we own the Voice, instead of letting it affect us in unexpected ways. This work can also be thought of as shadow work. We bring the shadow aspect into the light a little bit through dialogues. It can also be done through art, music and other means. The dialogues are a powerful way to work with the shadow aspects. It takes a little shift in perspective. But it's very healthy. When I do this work on retreats, it some-times starts slow. Once the practitioner locks in the voice, however, the voices just flow. I've witnessed many profound insights with practitioners who do this work.

Aspects of Self: Fear of Power

Here is an example to illustrate how the Fear of Power, as one of the aspects, may speak. Read through it, speaking out loud, to get the feeling of how the practice works. This is just an example. You'll need to do your own work to gain the benefit.

1. I am the Voice that Fears Power.
2. I see the world as a threat.
3. My job is to protect the Self from anything and everything.
4. What am I afraid of? Anything that can hurt us!
5. I serve the Self by keeping him from becoming a victim. Any time something gives off the hint of power, whatever the form, I send a signal.
6. If I have to, I can hit the full-scale red alert button. Don't make me go DEFCON!
7. Nobody's going to hurt us while I'm on board.
8. Why do I exist? They took advantage of the Self when he was too small to do anything about it.
9. Any power scares me.
10. I still feel like a Victim when people talk about a Higher Power.
11. I fear power because I have no trust.
12. There hasn't been enough evidence in my life that anyone is worth trusting.
13. The easiest thing to do is to get out of the way, or give people what they want.

14. I avoid situations where the self is called to have power. It's too risky to take responsibility.
15. I protect the self from being taken advantage of.
16. It's better to lay low and play it safe than to be consumed by something larger.

Aspects of Self

Who are you?

_____

_____

_____

What is your job?

_____

_____

_____

How do you serve the whole self?

_____

_____

_____

How do you hinder the self?

_____

_____

_____

Closing Steps

1. After processing with an archetypal voice, it's important to let the energy settle.
2. Avoid popping up and going about the day.
3. Give yourself at least a few minutes to regroup.
4. Visualize your aspect, in this case the one that fears power, sitting in front of you.
5. Send light, love, and compassion towards it.
6. Know that all of these are parts of you, parts of the greater collective.
7. Reintegrate the energy before proceeding by imagining beams of healing light returning to your heart.
8. If another type of visualization works better for you, use it. If something comes up naturally, learn to use that in your meditation. There's a reason why it's natural.

Dedication

May the merits of this practice be of benefit to those who suffer. May we all be free of suffering and the cause of suffering. May all beings know happiness and the cause of happiness.

Reflections

_____

_____

_____

_____

_____

_____

The Vows

6

In Buddhism there are many types of vows and multiple interpretations of what they are; how they must be taken; what preliminary practices are required; how they're upheld; what happens if we break them; and how to purify before; during and after taking vows. In the original schools of Buddhism, vows were meant for *monastics: monks and nuns.* I'm not an expert in these. In fact, they're so complicated and the material on them is so dense, it seems that it would take a lifetime of commitment to study and master them. These were the tools of a committed renunciate. I'm not a monk and have no interest in becoming a monk. I do consider myself a neo-monastic, however. I'll talk about how the average person can understand and use Buddhist Vows in everyday life outside of monastic traditions. These are some of the vows that I've taken and that I try to uphold. I think this is practical and within reach of Westerners like myself who are in recovery. As always, looking at Buddhism through the eyes of the addict should also be enlightening for the non-addict.

General Types of Buddhist Vows

<u>Refuge Vows:</u> Refuge in Buddha (Teacher), Dharma (Teaching), and Sangha (Community). These are always done first. None of the other vows or tantric initiations can be taken without taking refuge first.

<u>Monastic Vows:</u> For becoming a monk or nun. These are very complex and detailed. See the *Path of Purification,* Vinaya texts for all you've ever wanted to know about monasticism.

<u>Lay Vows:</u> For non-monastics to refrain from harming; lying; stealing; sexual misconduct; and/or taking of intoxicants. These can be taken separately or all together for life or for any time period.

<u>Bodhisattva Vows:</u> To practice Dharma for the sake of all beings. These include the promise not to become fully enlightened until every single suffering being is saved. Bodhisattvas progress along ten grounds or stages.

<u>Tantric Vows:</u> All of the preceding vows, plus those relating to the Guru and the tantric community of practitioners. The tantric vows are made on an energy level and are part of a tantric initiation process.

All of the preceding vows take place in the physical realm and end with the death of our physical
body. But the tantric vows continue throughout
reincarnations and only end when we reach full
enlightenment. On the tantric path, enlightenment is said to be achievable anywhere from one
to twenty-one lifetimes. The previous paths take
much longer, but are more accessible. The tantric
vows are also called samaya. When we break
tantric vows we're said to have broken samaya.

In this book we'll focus mostly on Refuge Vows
and Lay Vows. I've written more on the principles
of a Bodhisattva in *The 12-Step Buddhist*. Before
we look at these in detail, let's frame our practice in the context of recovery. As we practice
recovery from a 12-Step perspective, we want to
think about refuge in the context of our 11th Step,
"Sought through prayer and meditation to improve
our conscious contact with God as we understand
God, praying only for knowledge of His will for us
and the power to carry that out."

With a little filtering, it's not so difficult to work
with this in a non-theistic manner. Below are some
examples. But don't feel limited by these. Try to
understand the process of *reframing: rethinking in
a more useful way* and come up with your own
system for making it work. Or borrow mine. As
long as you understand what you're doing, it's fine.

- Prayer: commitment; refuge; respect;
  surrender; asking; affirming; seeking; or
  knowing. Every serious thought is a prayer.
- Meditation: study; reflection; discussion;
  recitation; or concentration.
- Conscious contact: presence; awareness;
  feeling something deeper; joy; serenity;

recognition; body sensation; emotional awareness; or watching our thoughts.

- God: the Now; this instant; our life; our heart; our creation; manifestation; experience; celebration; gratitude; principles of compassion; equanimity.
- His Will: All of the above, especially compassion; wisdom; fruition of meditation; maintaining of sacred vows; practice of the principles of the 12 Steps; Buddhism and other traditions which promote selfless service.

Reflections

What are some of your own filters for the more religious words used in 12-Step?

_____

_____

_____

_____

_____

_____

_____

When we seek through prayer, as some Buddhists do, we recite various sets of prayers or mantras, such as the Heart Sutra. Or, we can ask Buddha for help. Some people do that. It's worth a try. But to improve our conscious contact, from a Buddhist perspective, is to become aware, at deeper and deeper levels, of the aspects of our existence: body; energy; and mind. In Tibetan, the word for meditation is _gompa: familiarize_. Conscious contact means to become familiar. When we become familiar with the impermanent, changing, empty nature of our experience, we gain wisdom. Through that wisdom we gain power—the power to practice compassion. That's the real power of vow: to remove our obstacles to happiness. True happiness is a special level of compassion.

When we meditate on the 11th step like this, we can sit comfortably on our cushion, or a park bench, even in 12-Step meetings. We can eventually learn to bring our practice into other places—even where people are speaking about their Higher Power as something external.

We don't have to use the Dharma as an excuse to feel superior. In fact, we can understand that the mainstream views in AA, NA, or religion are beneficial steps in the conscious evolution of humanity. His Holiness the Dalai Lama says that it doesn't really matter if we're religious or not. The non-believer should

> *The most important thing about being a Dharma practitioner or a 12-Step Buddhist is to match our ideals with our actions.*

still be able to understand the principle and benefit of compassion and human affection. These are basic to the human experience. Compassion came first. Religions came later. So it's entirely irrelevant if we happen to consider ourselves religious or not when it comes to compassion. As I've said many times, Buddhism is a science of mind. I don't think of it as a religion. But some people do, and that's okay.

If we really have an evolved view, then we can remain relaxed and helpful in the presence of people with different views. But not if we bullshit ourselves into thinking we're superior in our minds, holding resentment in our hearts while we meditate with a smug look on our faces. The most important thing about being a Dharma practitioner or a 12-Step Buddhist is to match our ideals with our actions. In other words, walk the walk. Don't give Buddhism a bad name by being a dick, just as you wouldn't want to drive like a maniac with an Easy Does It AA sticker on your bumper. We may be the only Big Book (AA basic text) or Buddhist that someone ever sees. Represent!

Refuge Vows:

"The five general precepts are not to renounce the Three Jewels, even at the expense of one's life or country; to put one's trust exclusively in the Three Jewels, without seeking worldly means, however great the necessity or importance, to make offerings regularly to the Three Jewels on the prescribed occasions, with a constant appreciation of their qualities; to go for refuge with an awareness of the benefits of doing, and to encourage others to do the same and to prostrate before the Buddhas and depictions of them wherever one happens to be." –Jamgon Kongtrul

- I take refuge in the Buddha
  NAMO BUDDAYA.
- I take refuge in the Dharma
  NAMO DHARMAYA.
- I take refuge in the Sangha
  NAMO SANGHAYA.

We can chant the Refuge Vows in English or in Sanskrit, which I've added in parentheses. Namo: means homage or paying respect. For example, NAMO BUDDAYA means something like "I honor and respect the Buddha," and is used to recite the first refuge vow. In the same way, we honor and respect the Dharma with NAMO DHARMAYA, and NAMO SANGHAYA for the communities of practitioners. Note: communities are plural. We respect every tradition, no matter how different it may appear from our own. There's a special melody for singing this prayer that I received from Khachab Rinpoche. If you'd like to learn it, there's a video at www.thepowerofvow.com.

Some use the word prayer when chanting the refuge vows. Refuge vows are considered to be similar. It depends on our sense of prayer. If we see the Buddha as something outside of ourselves that we are praying to, maybe it's accurate to call it a prayer. This outer view is dualistic. It's better to be dualistic with a sacred object of refuge than something negative. Ultimately we need to transcend dualistic thinking. But maybe that's not where we're at in the moment. It's okay. Be where you are. Practice where you stand.

Practice where you stand.

We can also view the refuge as something inside ourselves. If we consider, in our meditation, that our Buddha nature is inseparable from our inner dimension, we can take refuge internally. Maybe this is too difficult, but we may feel some sense of it. In that case, it's still more of a prayer than a *siddhi: realization*. It may feel like we're saying, "I pray to realize my Buddha nature within." That works. It's important to understand that there are different levels and meanings of prayer.

The Buddha, Dharma and Sangha are called the Three Jewels. Refuge in the Three Jewels forms the cornerstone of any Buddhist practice. First we should understand what it means to take refuge. To take refuge doesn't necessarily mean that we hide from something. The 12-Step Buddhist faces life on life's terms. But sometimes we pull back from our own will into the Buddha Voice—the Voice of the Teachings. Put another way, refuge is simply the action of taking shelter from our suffering.

Maybe we don't feel like we're suffering in this moment. Things could seem relatively okay. But most people come to Dharma practice, like recovery, because of some problems, or struggles. We spend so much time covering up our cycles of suffering, with addictions, distractions, intentions and actions. Once we begin to peel the onion, however, patterns come to light. As we say in the 12-Step community, more will be revealed.

What does it mean to seek shelter from our suffering? It doesn't mean that we avoid it. It means that we should understand our condition and choose different actions than those that cause more suffering. But we need to examine our state closely. That's what mediation is. Recently a woman in our 12-Step Buddhist group complained of severe back pain all the time. She had a way of "checking out" when she meditated with her eyes closed. To take refuge in the Buddha means to have the courage to go right into the middle of our suffering. It doesn't mean that we have to do it all at once, but we can make incremental explorations into our pain. I suggested that she try it for a few moments at a time, meditating with her eyes open, allowing herself to safely explore the sensations briefly with a sense of curiosity. She found this useful, but it was a very different approach, and an understandable defense mechanism from pain.

As addicts, we don't naturally want to feel what we feel. Our nature is to change what we feel with our drugs of choice—whatever form they take. When we're clean and sober, our brains may find other ways to medicate. It's part survival mechanism and part addictive response and is definitely related to trauma. The Buddha asks us to go into our suffering. This is the opposite action to our normal response. If we practice this way, we're already entering the path. But I don't consider it going against the stream.

What we resist persists.

What we resist persists. The best way to approach pain management using Buddhist tools is to learn to relax deeply. That might involve some techniques that aren't traditionally Buddhist or aren't typically discussed in the lower schools of Buddhism. For that reason, I suggested that this woman try a breathing technique, similar to the one used in the practice sections of this book. When she tried this, she reported even more of a shift in consciousness.

As a yoga practitioner, I use directed breathing practice constantly. For many years, as a Zen practitioner, I only used breath awareness practice. The difference is that in yoga we control the breath and in Zen we leave the breath as it is. We don't direct it, we observe it. It's actually cool to use both of these. It's similar to taking a yoga class. In Vinyasa Yoga we often direct the breathing for most of the class until we get to our *savasana: final resting pose*. Then we switch to the awareness only approach, letting the breathing resume its organic state. We can also apply this in our sitting meditation practice.

There are many ways to meditate. It's not always about watching our breath. We read Dharma, apply methods, and consider the effects. Study is meditation. Ethics are meditation. Vows are application. Application is meditation. Meditation is familiarization. From this state of becoming familiar with how life is we can gain insight. Insights occur on many levels but lead to wisdom. Wisdom is the deep knowledge of our real condition. Instead of being slaves to our senses, thoughts, impulses, the desires of others, we simply watch as it all unfolds. This is sometimes referred to as a Magical Display. That's a different point of view than ignorance. Ignorance is bullshit. The Dharma is badass. It begins with refuge. From my vantage point, nothing is more important than refuge.

We may or may not have direct experience or a whole lot of faith that the Buddha was really an enlightened being. We certainly may have strange ideas on what it means to be enlightened. None of them are accurate. Enlightenment is not an idea. It's not based on mind, but is beyond mind. Note: mind doesn't like hearing that and will rebel. This is an archetype. The enlightened state is not mind, but is the nature of mind. There are many paths to help us get into this knowledge on a direct,

> *Study is meditation. Ethics are meditation. Vows are application. Application is meditation. Meditation is familiarization.*

experiential and practical basis. As it says in the AA literature: the spiritual life is not a theory, it has to be lived. But we need a theory for a frame of reference to initiate us into practice.

The framework is called the view. We might call our Dharma view 'right view,' from the Eightfold Path. There are many views and subsequently many teachings and methods to establish the respective views. Ultimately all views will be abandoned. But if we say that too early, without direct experience, we're blowing spiritual smoke. That won't pay off so well.

It is said that as a Buddha in training, a Bodhisattva can manifest in 100 bodies simultaneously for the benefit of beings. Fully enlightened Buddhas can manifest in millions of bodies in different dimensions for the benefit of beings. We can think about ourselves as enlightened all day long, especially if we've had some spiritual awakenings, whether they're white light experiences or simply moments of relative clarity. But we should read the texts that describe the miraculous qualities of Buddhas. These can be a source of inspiration— and a reality check.

We should understand that it is due to our lack of faith and lack of understanding that we need to seek refuge. The power of vow is the power of refuge. We need a little faith to enter onto the path. Faith is simply confidence. Confidence is good in any amount. Jesus mentioned that all we needed was faith the size of a mustard seed. It

> *We're already experts at taking refuge in many things, mainly our egos.*

doesn't take a lot to start. Remember, seeds grow into trees given the right conditions. Think about the power of karma, and the exponential growth potential of a single action. Should we wait until we're spiritually fit enough to take refuge? That would be the same kind of bad logic that says we should wait until we're skinny to go on a diet.

Should we spend our lives trying to become a good enough person to feel worthy of refuge? Nope. We should come as we are to the place of refuge. What do we take refuge in? We can look at it in many ways.

We're already experts at taking refuge in many things, mainly our egos. The ego is necessary for us to function in the world. But on the spiritual path the ego gets in the way. The ego doesn't want to dissolve into emptiness. It wants to survive and perpetuate its existence. In Dharma practice, we first shift our power from the ego to refuge in the Buddha. This transforms our relationship to our personal power.

Reflections

_____

_____

_____

_____

_____

_____

I Take Refuge in Buddha

Perhaps we ask for help in the form of a prayer. It's a start. The refuge prayer itself can be the refuge. The act of taking refuge means that we're seeking wisdom higher than our own egoic nature, as Eckhart Tolle calls it. Taking refuge in the Buddha is really about turning inward. We learn to tap into our Buddha potential so that we can start listening to that voice instead of our ego. This step in refuge gives us new power to make different choices in our thoughts and actions.

"I take refuge in the Buddha
The realm of the Buddhas is inconceivable;
No sentient being can fathom it...
The Buddhas constantly emit great beams of light:
In each light beam are innumerable Buddhas...
The Buddha-body is pure and always tranquil;
The radiance of its light extends throughout the world;
The Buddha's freedom cannot be measured-
It fills the cosmos and all space...
The Buddha body responds to all – none do not see it.
With various techniques it teaches the living,
Sound like thunder, showering the rain of truth...
All virtuous activities in the world
Come from the Buddha's light."
–Avatamsaka Sutra, in *Mahayana Buddhism* by Paul Williams

The practice of taking refuge in the Buddha means that we understand something of the truth of suffering. Once we understand a little more deeply about how we suffer, we can apply the first level of refuge. First things first. We take refuge for our own sake to find a path out of our own suffering. When we practice in the *Mahayana: great vehicle*, we take refuge not only for our own sake but for the sake of others as well.

As I mentioned above, first, we can take outer refuge in the external idea or image of a Buddha. We can also take refuge in our own internal Buddha qualities. Caveat: we act on our refuge vows by practicing the prefect qualities of a Buddha. As we say in 12-Step, the spiritual life is not a theory. Right? It's different from making a prayer request and waiting for good fortune to fall from the sky. Instead we practice what the Tibetans call, "enlightenment in the palm of our hands." See *Perfect Practice* for instructions on how to work with the qualities, called *paramitas: perfections,* in ourselves and with others.

We can also take secret refuge: beyond words and concepts, in our own Buddha nature, which requires teachings that we won't get into here. One way to talk about Buddha nature is as the infinite space in which everything happens. It's our home. We're already there. There's nowhere to go, nothing to achieve. We can't change, fix, alter, break or modify the *Dharmakaya: enlightened state of pure wisdom.* Taking this kind of refuge is a deep level of practice and requires transmission from a qualified Master in order to become a sustainable practice that can be developed into an ongoing state of being. That said we might get glimpses along the way. Perhaps we've had many of these in our life, even before we became interested in any spiritual path. It's similar to being "in the zone" when we're concentrating on a project, making love, engaging in intense physical activity, doing yoga, playing music or simply looking at the sky. The difference between occasionally getting into or near the zone and the path of liberation is that the path, with practice, puts us permanently in the Buddha zone. It takes a deeper level of concentration than average experience. This is developed through years, if not lifetimes, of practice.

> "Within the seed of mindfulness is the seed of concentration.
> With these two energies, we can liberate ourselves from afflictions." Thich Nat Hanh

Whatever our capacity and wherever we are when we step on to the path of refuge is a step into the Buddha Zone. When we take Buddhist refuge, regardless of the level of our practice in a given moment, we are walking the path. The Buddha said to practice mindfulness at the Four Moments; sitting, standing, sleeping, eating. The Buddha Zone has layers, just like our consciousness. Sometimes we're awake, sometimes asleep, sometimes in deep sleep. Being in the Buddha Zone is also being in the refuge in every moment, or as often as we can remember!

The Buddha said to practice mindfulness at the Four Moments; sitting, standing, sleeping, eating.

Traditionally, there are some rules that go along with taking refuge. According to some traditions, one must take formal refuge to be a Buddhist. Following refuge, he or she is not to venerate "worldly deities." It sounds a little like when the Bible says, "You shall have no Gods before me." Exodus 20:3. I think a lot of people in general and people in recovery specifically like the idea of being Buddhist. Some might even call themselves Buddhist because they like something they read or because they identify with certain teachings. Many seem to lump Buddha in with all the other spiritual figures. They might say "Buddha, Jesus, and Mohammed," all in the same sentence, as if they're the same figure. The Buddhist teachings however are very specific, detailed and quite different from anything else. There are of course commonalities. And the Dalai Lama often says that all religions share the same principles. But the deeper explanations reveal some extremely unique teachings. One reason that I write these books is to help people understand these similarities and the differences.

Reflections

What is the difference between a creator God and the Buddha?

_____

_____

_____

_____

_____

_____

I was in a noon 12-Step meeting recently where a girl shared how she rejected the Judeo-Christian aspect of the 12 Steps. She mentioned Buddhism, which technically we're not supposed to do in recovery groups. "But I'm not a Buddhist either," she said. As if Buddhism was somehow just as bad as any other religion. I've said it elsewhere, I don't think of Buddhism as a religion. Many do. But there seems to be a block against commitment amongst people in recovery. They're often afraid to commit to anything beyond meetings and the traditional program of recovery. Those who move beyond that stage, however, seem to be happier, healthier people.

One of the other rules of refuge is to not affiliate with religious extremists. That probably means that we should follow the Middle Way in all things, even and especially Dharma practice. Among other obligations of one who has taken refuge is that we are to regard "as if it were the actual Three Jewels" and treat respectfully any representation of the Buddha. This includes words, books, images, "even a single letter," or as much as a patch of yellow cloth," according to Jamgon Kongtrul. That means you wouldn't put your Dharma book, mala, or image of the Buddha on a chair. Would you put Buddha's face where people's butts go? That's the logic. We don't even let our sacred books touch the ground but rather put a pillow or fancy cloth down first.

Here's how I practice with this one. To venerate the Buddha is to take refuge. It's more like humility than worship. Any time that I see a representation of the Buddha, in any form, I try to make an offering of refuge. I might do this mentally, by thinking, "OM AH HUM." May I achieve total liberation for the benefit of all beings." If I'm in a situation where it won't make people uncomfortable, I put my hands together at heart center and say something like that. Sometimes I walk by the books in my Dharma library and just bow my head for a moment. Other times I ask myself, "What would Buddha do?"

Another way to take refuge is to put our hands together at heart center or atop our heads, blessing the crown chakra, then the third eye (between the eyebrows), then throat and heart and say,

"To the Bhagavan, Tatagatha, Victorious One, Conqueror Shakyamuni Buddha, I prostrate, make offerings and go for refuge."

Then we might do a full prostration all the way to the belly, or a simple bowing of the head.

Reflections

What are your thoughts and feelings about refuge in the Buddha?

_____

_____

_____

_____

_____

_____

_____

I take refuge in the Dharma

The term Dharma has many definitions in Hinduism and various branches of Buddhism. The way it was explained to me in an undergrad course on the History of Buddhism was that there are "little d" dharmas and "big D" Dharma. Little d dharmas comprise the vast universe of conditioned phenomena. In some traditions these are numbered seventy-two, in others eighty-one. The *conditioned phenomena are physical; earth, air, fire, water, mental; moral and immoral views, consciousness; instantly arising, and falling perceptions.* These constituents are dependent on karma, are impermanent, and are illusory. These are the dharmas in the Pali Canon, which is the record of what Buddha taught. It was kept in memory by some monks and was written down hundreds of years after he died. When Buddhas die, Buddhists say they passed to *parinirvana: enlightenment.*

Big D Dharma is the doctrine of the Buddha. But which school, teacher, system, group has the real, super-Big-B-for-Buddha teachings, and which are false? These are good questions. I will try to avoid answering them. That said, we could follow our guts and try to do our best to find good teachers. Ultimately, we must be our own teachers. As Joko Beck would say, "Life, just as it is, the only teacher." Does that mean we don't need a teacher in the flesh? I don't think so.

The Zen Masters and Tibetan Lamas: Tibetan Dharma teachers that I've worked with have been invaluable at showing me what I needed to see. They have a way of exposing to the student their ego, limitations, and attachments. When we push or demand something, whether it's an answer to a question, or attention, we're probably not going to get it. Anyone who's spent time with a guru knows how this can be. A good friend of mine is a long term, fully ordained nun. She has many stories of how the teachings have been delivered in ways that were not according to her desires. But our obscurations are so deep, so prevalent, there's no way we're going to penetrate into our own core truth without some help. It's so easy to delude ourselves and give in to our egoic attachments.

It's very helpful, especially for addicts, to have someone to check ourselves against. That's why we have 12-Step sponsors to help us get honest when we work through the steps. We learn to respect what our sponsor says or we'll have to find another one. Good sponsors don't take any BS. Similarly, whomever we choose to take Dharma teachings from is our teacher in that moment and should be respected as such. If we have a falling out later, we should still pay respect and move along on our path without too much criticism. This is a different practice than we find in AA, where gossip and slander are common. Addicts are narcissistic and over sensitive. We get big resentments quickly and easily and have a tendency to share those feelings within the community. This kind of practice will get us nowhere in Buddhist sanghas.

If we think of how addicted we are to conditioned phenomena, be it of body, speech or mind, we can see the patterns of attachment and aversion. Note that in the abhidarma kosha body of literature, even good morals are considered to be little d dharmas— conditioned factors—that we take as ultimate. Somehow we need to see through the illusory quality of our own beliefs, no matter how high and mighty they may be. There's a reality that is not conditioned. Dharma teaches us how to know that reality,

> *Somehow we need to see through the illusory quality of our own beliefs, no matter how high and mighty they may be.*

sometimes called nirvana, or nibbana, in a nondual sense. We can take refuge in the teachings, though they too are part of conditioned existence.

Eventually we're "gone, gone, gone, to the other shore," realizing we'd never left. A commentary on the Prajnaparamita Sutra states,

> "The Dharma should be attained as nothing to settle in and nothing to grasp."

What we mean here by dharma is the teachings of the Buddha. That said, if we understand the similarities and differences between Buddhist teachings and other teachings, we could also take refuge in "other," non-Buddhist Dharma. Note: this is considered heresy by some. We can easily find people who disagree with this, and that's okay. This is how I practice. Choose for yourself. But if we are able to understand with some clarity the essential meaning of spiritual teachings and have the sharpness to draw the distinctions, without watering anything down or mixing it all up in a Dharma salad, we can take refuge in all Dharmas. It's a bit advanced to think this way. Some people call themselves things like "Integral" and think they understand how to draw everything together into a soup. It's not so easy to do that. But it can be done.

Be wise about who you listen to. Do your research. Buddhism is different. Traditions within Buddhism vary in their views. Christianity and Taoism are not the same as Buddhism. People like to say that it doesn't matter what you call it, it's all the same. It's not all the same. Deep in the essence, if we have that ability, we can see what is the same. But there are differences. If we really understand the Dharma, we can find the truth everywhere. I hope that's not too confusing. The knowledge of this is more of a heart thing than a head thing.

There are many lineages and schools all over the world. There are stages and levels of teachings. We don't have to automatically take refuge in every teaching. But we can respect them. Most people can only handle being in one group and that's okay. The vow to take refuge in the Dharma may look like taking refuge in one book, one school, one sutra, or one teacher. Or not.

I walk a lot of lines and cross a lot of paths. I know many practitioners who can't handle that. You don't have to be like me. If we choose only one branch, we may be narrow-minded. Plus, if we don't settle on one, we may be non-committal. Regardless of the branch or branches of Dharma that we follow, we should pay respect to the others. I've found that most people, including Buddhists and addicts, have a tendency to be non-integral. They stick to their niches. It's a social dynamic to pay allegiance to the flag of our nation, or gang, family, home group, corporate softball team or Buddhist sangha. The Dalai Lama defines secular in classical Indian terms as inclusive of all religions and non-believers. That's a pretty spiritual view! And it's a deep level of practicing the vow of refuge in the Dharma.

Taking refuge in the Dharma may mean practicing respect for teachings or an apparent lack of teachings in others.

Reflections

Have you ever thought of refuge like this? What do you feel Dharma is and why would you seek refuge in the Dharma?

_____

_____

_____

_____

_____

_____

_____

Dharma can bring some comfort and relief at first. But it's not about the comfort zone. Dharma is usually the last thing the ego wants to take refuge in. Taking refuge in the Dharma may mean that we practice respect for the unique dimensions of everyone, regardless of how difficult that is. If we want to call ourselves Buddhists, that's fine. But does that mean we have to criticize and disagree with other Buddhists, Christians, 12-Steppers, people who don't have the slightest idea about anything spiritual? No, being a Buddhist does not mean that. Taking refuge in the Dharma may mean keeping our mouths shut in meetings, at the Thanksgiving Pot Luck or family gathering.

As I mentioned in *The 12-Step Buddhist*, the Buddha can be seen as the doctor. The Dharma is our medicine. Sometimes we don't like to take our medicine. When we're children we might take some sugary, fruit flavored cough syrup. When I was a child, I'd hold my nose when taking some bad tasting stuff meant to cure my ills. Sometimes the Dharma might not go down so easily. Then we reject the refuge. We may subconsciously reject our refuge many times daily. When we scrap our refuge, we discard the teaching, the teachers and the path. People in recovery understand this. We call it self-will run riot.

When we try to get sober, sometimes we wind up in a meeting or a treatment center. We arrive torn up, sick, confused, hopeless, and desperate. But when we start to feel better, we might get ideas about how things should be. The people in the meeting annoy us. The nurses ignore us. The doctor refuses to fill our prescription for pain meds. We don't get our cookie. We find all sorts of ways to reject the solution. It's a setup for relapse. The more dissatisfied we become, the more evidence we build into our case for getting loaded. The Addict wins. Below are a few ways that we practice not taking refuge in the Dharma:

- When we reject our chosen program, we move off the path of recovery and into the path of relapse. Every little step counts. We must be diligent!
- We try to take bits and pieces of the teaching.
- Focusing on what we like don't like. "Oh, I prefer this teacher's book, that teacher's sangha."
- "I'm Buddhist, but I don't believe in karma."

- "I accept the teachings on karma, but I can't get behind the whole past life thing."
- "I like the Dalai Lama, but I heard that he eats meat."
- "I'd go to the Dharma Center more often, but that one lady is so rude."

Because we reject refuge more often than we take refuge, the practice of repeating the vows at least three times daily is a good one.

Taking refuge in the Dharma really means doing practice. Practice can take different forms. Even if we're not sitting on our meditation cushion counting our breaths, there are ways to practice throughout the day. Sometimes just putting our hands together when we pass our altar is a pretty good way to reconnect with refuge. I have images, statues, books, prayer flags, mala beads and other such things all around the house. I try to keep a Buddha in sight in every direction. Wherever I look, I can take refuge. This might seem a little eccentric or excessive. But then again, Buddhism is an esoteric practice and frankly, samsara is excessive. Wuddya gonna do?

I dated a girl who, prior to meeting me, had no exposure to Buddhism. I introduced her to some teachings. She soon tuned into some online teachings. After one retreat, I noticed something odd. She'd set up her whole apartment the same way as I had mine in terms of altars, and images. She took it a step further: mantras written on the mirror. I went over there to visit and said, "Uh, this is kind of creepy. It looks like my place." I don't know if going from zero to gung-ho overnight is how we want to do it. If we're inspired, hey go for it. It can't hurt, especially if we're trying to be a serious practitioner.

But if we use the Dharma for other purposes, like to impress somebody, we're headed for trouble.

Once I had a Tibetan Lama stay at the house for a retreat we organized. I'd taken up the habit of wearing these beautiful Green Tara medallions. Whenever someone noticed one, I took it off and gave it to them. I thought it was a nice practice. I figured that if they had the karma to connect with the Dharma, I should give them my Green Tara! The Lama had a different view. He said that if you give Dharma items to people who don't respect the Dharma, it could create negative karma for them. So now I'm a little more careful. I give things away if people show interest, not just attraction to something shiny. Remember, karma requires the three aspects of intention, action, and satisfaction to bear fruit. If I have all three, and they have all three, who knows? Maybe somebody benefits. But if we fill our house with Tibetan images to impress our boyfriend, maybe it's not so good. Here's where mindfulness, tempered with self-honesty, can be helpful.

Another way to take refuge in the Dharma is to study the teachings. Go to retreats, talks, and teachings in other traditions. Visit centers in and out of our comfort zone. Read books. Listen to talks. Take a pilgrimage to see a teacher or a sacred site. Invite people to meditate but—remember don't proselytize. All of these things contribute to our sense of connecting with teaching. The teaching is the Dharma. We can connect at whatever level that our capacity allows. Maybe we get overwhelmed at all of the stuff going on in one center. So we might try something more low key. Later on we might find ourselves feeling under-stimulated. We're free to try something else. We should try to keep our refuge in our hearts. That's where it grows. That's where the vow takes hold, spreads roots and gives us strength.

We can practice Dharma in so many ways. We can use our body to practice generosity, our speech to sing mantras or speak kind words, our minds to visualize compassionate light rays reaching out to all beings that suffer. Again, this may seem like a little bit of mixing things to a particular tradition or view. But if we're clear on what we're doing, we can practice what we need to create healing for ourselves, and others.

Reflections

_____

_____

_____

_____

_____

_____

_____

_____

_____

_____

I take refuge in the Sangha

"A connected community provides its members with strength and safety. When we feel strong and safe, we can put our energy into evolving socially, culturally and spiritually." — Nicholas Boothman

Sangha means spiritual community. For our survival, humans have to rely on what sociologists consider the concentric circles—near to far—of support. In a conventional, non-Buddhist sense we don't normally call it so, but in some ways we already take refuge in our relationships with individuals, family, schools, teams, workgroups, social networks, and greater society. We rely on them for survival, growth, development, and self-definition. If we were to be a short time without these, I imagine we'd notice pretty quickly how deeply we're connected to institutions, city, state, and country.

If we suddenly found ourselves standing in the middle of a desert plain, with no buildings, streets, or people, we'd have to quickly become some kind of MacGyver-like super-survivalist just to make it through a day. We need our concentric circles to be connected to our life. We can take refuge in sangha without giving up any of these societal connections. But we begin to shift what we accept as important.

> *We can take refuge in sangha without giving up any of these societal connections.*

We still need money to meet basic needs, but when we take refuge, we may feel less driven by the need to accumulate wealth. And when it comes to conversations, we rely on our sangha for common ground that asks us to question all of our values, all of what we see as real—even our own sense of self. This is what changes. It's mostly internal, though external changes may become more apparent over time. We keep our jobs, do our daily tasks and practice our teachings. Nobody else needs to know. They might notice after a while that we're nicer, more patient, and less reactive. But it's very difficult to achieve these realizations as solitary practitioners. The support of a like-minded sangha, just like 12-Step groups, is extremely beneficial.

In fact, some teachers would say not to associate with those not on the path of Dharma. I can understand this perspective. It's very easy to get sidetracked into mundane, non-Dharmic thinking when we're engrossed and engaged in the material world of materialists and their obsessions. I spend so much time with spiritual seekers that it's second nature to me. But if I didn't have my 12-Step community and my Buddhist groups, it might become more and more difficult to keep my mind on the path and the path on my mind. Most of the world, sadly, is not on a spiritual plane. It's so easy to be addicted to samsara. Any addict can understand this. The non-addict, though not consuming heroin, is still a samsara junkie.

> *The non-addict, though not consuming heroin, is still a samsara junkie.*

When we begin to seriously study the teachings, we need support from others on the path. If we discuss a practice, such as *Tonglen: exchanging self for others*, we may find out pretty quickly that non-practitioners get mystified if we try to explain it. It's better if we keep quiet and work on ourselves and not get preachy about our Dharma practice.

Non-practitioners often have no idea what we're about as Buddhists, so we should be respectful of their views. We may come home from a particularly inspiring retreat only to find that our family feels like we've joined a cult. The same thing happens when addicts come home from treatment talking about God, the program, meditation and amends.

We should be careful with whom we share our spirituality. It's usually not appropriate to discuss spiritual beliefs and practices in the workplace. We therefore need to be cautious about how much we share outside of our sangha. My teacher often says that it's not good to make people feel uncomfortable. We're certainly not missionaries for Buddhism. One of our main practices is to pay respect to others. Repeat after me, **"I respect your beliefs."** Saying this a hundred times to ourselves, when we run into Christians, 12-Steppers and so on, instead of trying to prove how smart we are or how awesome our practice is, we can say, "I respect your beliefs," instead. That's a way to practice refuge in the Dharma. Try it.

When we take refuge in the Dharma, we shift focus to our spiritual community as support for our practice. As neo-monastics, we don't reject society. Of course we respect our families, workplaces and other groups, but we place special emphasis on learning and practicing Dharma with our fellow practitioners. This is pretty similar to the home group concept in 12-Step communities. I personally include 12-Step in my notion of sangha.

Some teachers support the idea of addicts having their own form of Buddhist recovery, as an alternative to regular 12-Step. They may say it's because some addicts can't tolerate the theistic language of 12-Step programs. While I agree that it makes sense to participate in Buddhist and other spiritual support systems for our recovery, I disagree about giving people an "out" when it comes to 12-Step. In my nearly 30 years of experience in 12-Step, Dharma and other groups, I can say that there's no better place to learn tolerance than a 12-Step community. But I try not to tell people what they should do. I used to insist that they go to 12-Step meetings if they wanted to come to my meditation group. My opinion is that 12-Step is irreplaceable. In long-term 12-Step involvement, we meet so many people and can form amazing relationships with depth, honesty, problems, and intensity. But some people won't go. I still think they can be helped, so I try not to push too much.

Reflections

What are your feelings about 12-Step groups?

_____

_____

_____

_____

_____

_____

_____

_____

_____

_____

If we can learn to integrate instead of alienate ourselves, we can fully own our Buddhist values in the 12-Step context. This is better than throwing the Buddha out with the bathwater. We might do that if we say that 12-Step has no value because Buddhists have no god. There are gods in Buddhism. They're different than the Christian Creator God concept. But along with other tools, Buddhist deities, such as those found in Tibetan Buddhism: Green Tara, Chenrezig, and Medicine Buddha, can be used as a higher power. The sangha in a 12-Step community can also be thought of as a higher power, especially if we surrender to the "group conscience" of a business meeting. Turn it over!

But sangha goes wider and deeper than the secular community. Consideration of sangha varies somewhat depending on the type of Buddhism. In some communities, we take refuge in a small group of people who attend the same meditation group. In the *Vajrayana: diamond vehicle* systems, we normally take initiations with large groups of dozens or more. I just took a long life initiation with His Holiness Sakya Trizin with over 500 Tibetans and a handful of Westerners. In that sense our sangha included everyone who took that initiation with us at that time, as well as anyone who had ever taken that initiation and everyone who will ever receive it. Our sangha is also comprised of the *Arya: Noble beings that have transcended the physical plane.*

Taking inner refuge in the sangha might mean seeing others as oneself. The practices of *metta: compassion, maitri: loving kindness, tonglen: exchanging self for others* all teach us ways to get in to this view. I spoke about some of these in previous works. These practices are quite difficult, and powerful.

From the safe confines of our in-group we tend to see things from a limited perspective. As an addict, or other egotist, I might see people outside of my local Dharma Punks group as, "outside the tradition," and therefore not, "one of us." If I follow a certain Tibetan Lama but not another Tibetan

Lama, I might think my sangha is better than their sangha. It's similar to going to a 12-Step meeting away from home. They never do it right! Right?

Reflections

Describe the group or groups that you belong to and those you do not belong to.

_____

_____

_____

_____

_____

_____

_____

_____

_____

I remember once I visited Boston and went to some 12-Step meetings. Unlike Portland, it was an all-volunteer format. No one got called on to share and there was no time limit. Instead, people shared as long as they wanted—sometimes more than 15 minutes! They all told their *drunk-a-logs: addiction war stories* instead of sharing on a specific topic like we do in Portland. At a meeting back home, I mentioned how different this was and made a little joke about it. Unbeknownst to me, there was a girl from Boston in the meeting. When she shared, she cussed me out at meeting level for "dissing" her town. I didn't mean to, and was just pointing out the differences. But it just reveals how we form our opinions on what's good and true and right based on the social systems that we spend our time in. To the Bostonians, their way is right. In Portland, our way seems best. Who's right? Both are right because we're all doing what we need to do. To take refuge in the sangha might mean to practice with this view.

The in-group out-group mentality is part of human nature. But in the dharma, we're trying to go beyond human nature to live in our Buddha nature. So it does us no good to be separatists. That's a lower level of thinking. It's higher than worshipping doorknobs I suppose. Integrate, don't separate.

Dharma asks us to go beyond our limitations. In some ways, this idea can be paradoxical. After all, a vow not to lie means we limit our speech. But the application of a limitation can show us how

"Make your limitation your un-limitation."

limited we are in another sense. I like what Bruce Lee said, "Make your limitation your un-limitation."

I've noticed a less than awesome phenomenon that happens at some Dharma groups. We sit for hours listening to teachings on something like compassion. When the teaching is over and the Lama leaves, some people seem to have a little bit of a Dharma glow or softer expression than when they walked. Then it's as if we're in a bus station trying to make it out of town. People snap right back into survival of the fittest mode. When I teach a meditation or yoga class, I ask people to be mindful of the transition "out" of meditation. Move smoothly and with grace. When the bell rings, try to transition mindfully, like a Zen monk in a forest monastery. Like a neo-monastic. Word.

Reflections

What is your ideal sangha?

_____

_____

_____

_____

_____

_____

_____

Practice Session: Refuge

As I've discussed elsewhere, we can think of
our recovery as our refuge. In our third step we
"turn it over" to a higher power or principle. That
is a form of refuge, even if they don't call it that in
12-Step. There are many ways that we seek refuge
in the material world. These things we are obsessed
with and addicted to be called the "inexhaustible
dharmas of conditioned existence." Knowing that
this is the situation for all conscious beings, in
Buddhism we intentionally seek refuge in the Three
Jewels of Buddha, Dharma, and Sangha. These are
also relative. But with wisdom we can learn how our
refuge in the sacred yet relative aspects of the Three
Jewels can lead us to total liberation.

Before we begin the session, let's think about the
refuge vows in terms of our inner voices or archetypes. The vows will be in opposition to some of the
dominant archetypes in our lives. When we take a
vow, these voices will boil up within us. That will
make it very difficult to keep vows. To let some of
that energy out, we'll speak in the first person as
one of these voices.

In this practice, we'll meditate, and then with the clarity gained from the meditation, we'll speak as the "Mind that Seeks Refuge." I've listed some sample questions and possible answers. These are my examples. Use them, or come up with your own. In addition to speaking as the voice, it's also interesting to simply sit in meditation as the Mind that Seeks Refuge. We can then try to notice what we're really taking refuge in— most likely a concept. What would it be like to take refuge, not in a concept, but in the infinite space of awakened mind? There's a difference, and while we might not be able to fully find this refuge, the first step will be to take notice of how we are taking refuge in our mind, rather than something beyond mind. To notice that difference requires the power of the refuge vow to still our minds long enough to see it.

Set a time for your session. There are free meditation timer apps for many smartphones. The formula for a practice session can be:

- Set Intention
- Breathe
- Sit
- Meditate
- Dialogue
- Dedicate

What do you want to achieve by doing this practice?

_____

_____

_____

_____

_____

It's your choice. Some people want a calm mind, or better focus, or clarity on some problem. Remember that all of these mundane problems are part of samsara. We'll never totally outrun them all. For all the problems that we can solve in mundane existence, an infinite number will continue to arise. This is the difference between serious Buddhist practice and something more self-oriented. Buddhism is never about building up the self. For this reason, we should try to make our intention something beyond self. An example might be, "I'm doing this session to fully realize my Buddha nature. May this Dharma work be of benefit in the liberation of all beings from suffering, and the root of suffering." The wording is optional.

Breathing

Do some breathing practice. Remember, this can be simple. Breathe in more deeply than normal. Exhale slowly and completely. Pause before you inhale and exhale.

Sitting

The basic principle is to sit, but what we do when we sit can vary greatly. In a refuge practice, we should build the "refuge field." Feel free to make it your own. In fact, it has to be something that you connect with to work in my opinion. To begin, imagine all of your relations seated with you. These can be your immediate family, extended family, aunts, and uncles—whatever comes to you. The range and number of our relations that we visualize here is limited only by your imagination. Consider openly their joys, their sufferings, their struggles and achievements. Once you have a sense, whether it's a good visualization or a feeling, and then add the "objects of refuge."

The objects of refuge are Buddhas, fully enlightened beings. It can be helpful to have statues or images of Buddhas or other objects of refuge such as saints or deities in front of you. But this practice is more about sense. Try to generate the visual ideas, but go with the feeling.

Imagine that in the space before you and above you are all of your relatives that you already generated, with infinite Buddhas that fill the sky. Any amount of detail that is natural is good enough. If you can, try to think about, see or feel their faces, compassionate smiles, and looks of enlightened contentment. Droplets of warm, loving energy in the form of lights rain down from the hearts of all the Buddhas. Lights are falling on everyone in the scene. The beams are absorbed into the heart centers of all who are present.

Again, if visualizing is too difficult, just go with the feelings generated by this imagery. How does it make you feel to think that Buddhas filled with compassion shine their heart lights and rain their blessings down on everyone that you love? The point is to have that intention, not to stress yourself out over the details. It's enough to have the thought and a general sense of the refuge field and the objects of refuge. It actually creates a lot of merit just to try! Now that we're in the space and intention of refuge, we can do a bit of focused meditation.

Next, pick your object of concentration; breath, body or sound. Pick one of those and commit to it for the duration of the practice session. It may be confusing to go back and forth between different objects of meditation for the first twenty years or so. Meditate by placing attention on your object of choice for a set amount of time; 5-15 minutes. For example, if you choose sound, just listen. When thoughts arise, recognize them as just thoughts, and then go back to listening. If you choose physical experience, just notice the sensations in your body. If you're working with the breath, you can either choose to notice where the breath enters the nose, or you can continue to work with one of the more directed breathing practices.

Whenever your mind drifts away from the object of meditation, bring your attention back to it. The practice of focusing on an object is called mindfulness. The practice of returning to the object once the mind drifts is called vigilance. We use both vigilance and mindfulness on the path, returning again and again. The process itself has many benefits on physical, emotional and mental levels. Now that we've settled our energy and focused our minds, we'll be in a good place to do some voice dialogues.

> *The practice of focusing on an object is called mindfulness.*

Aspects of Self: The Mind That Seeks Refuge

Next, we'll shift in to an Aspect of Self practice. As the Mind that Seeks Refuge, consider the following questions. Note: this practice can be done more than once and in different ways. Let this section be a guideline. Consider the question as the particular voice. There are examples provided, but for the work to have an effect, you'll need to answer your own way. Feel free to come up with your own question, or ask a sponsor, therapist or friend to help.

To shift into the aspect of the Voice that Seeks Refuge we say:

Who are you?
Example: I am the Mind that Seeks Refuge.

_____

_____

_____

As the Mind that Seeks Refuge, what are you really after?
Example: I'm looking for shelter. I need to protect the Self.

_____

_____

_____

What do you think of as refuge?
Example: I seek of a place to go that is safe, warm and comfortable.

_____

_____

_____

What kinds of things have you tried, in your effort to find refuge?
Example: I've tried drugs, alcohol, sex, relationships, financial prosperity, anger, pride, and greed.

_____

_____

_____

Where can the mind go?

_____

_____

_____

Is there a place?

_____

_____

_____

What will you do when you find what you're looking for?

_____

_____

_____

Who can help you on your quest?

_____

_____

_____

What kinds of things do you take refuge in that are not helpful?

_____

_____

_____

What will happen to you when you find the refuge that you seek?

_____

_____

_____

Aspects of Self:
The Voiceless Voice of Refuge

These are my own examples. Feel free to answer these questions verbally, in paint, on the guitar or another non-verbal manner. Perhaps just sit with the question mark.

Who are you?
I am Awakened Mind, the Voiceless Voice that is the Refuge of all suffering beings who seek enlightenment.

_____

_____

_____

What is your job?
There is no task, no goal, and no seeker, nothing sought. No observer, nothing to observe. Nothing is broken, therefore there is nothing to fix. Seekers take refuge in me. But I am nowhere else other than everywhere, so this enlightenment project leads nowhere.

_____

_____

_____

Are you the object of refuge?
All phenomena are objects of refuge. I am Present in all things

_____

_____

_____

How can we take refuge?

Be Present as the non-duality of infinite space. If that's too hard, seek lower paths.

_____

_____

_____

Lay Vows

8

"The days of shuck'n and jiv'n are over. ¬John P."

Refuge vows are pretty powerful. But to live the principles of refuge, we need to go further. The lay vows are the next level for a serious practitioner. The lay vows are for laypeople, referred to as house-holders in the old books. Monks didn't own houses or have family responsibilities. I'm assuming you're a layperson. If you were a monastic you wouldn't be reading my book because you probably know more about vows than I ever will. So for those of us who want to practice Dharma but are not interested in becoming full-fledged monks and nuns our vows are known as the *Pratimoksha: Vows of Personal Liberation*, which in Sanskrit means: *prati: personal or individual and moksha: liberation* . These are also sometimes referred to as just "Precepts in Zen," or the "Five Wonderful Precepts" as discussed by the Zen monk and prolific writer Thich Nhat Hanh.

Though personal and individual in their scope, the intention behind the Lay Vows is not selfish. We should be clear about this before embarking on the journey of being a vow holder. We practice for our own realization. When we become Buddhas, we will help others until samsara is completed. While we're working on ourselves, we can keep in mind that ultimately, we're going to become fully liberated, enlightened beings. Buddhas have limitless compassion to help those who suffer. That thought should always be part of our practice, whether we're laypeople, monks, addicts, or non-addicts.

The vows cover aspects of Body, Energy, and Mind. These are known as the "Three Gates" because they represent our centers of experience and aspects of our reality, which, though different, are inseparable. We can practice the *Nirmanakaya: physical path; Samboghakaya: the energy path*; and *Dharmakaya the mental path* (in Sanskrit). Teachings and teachers exist on all three levels. Sutra practice is on the physical level. The teachings of Shakyamuni Buddha work at this level of renunciation. There are also tantric practices that work on the energy level and Dzogchen practices are on the mind level. There are sets of vows associated with all of these different paths.

As we move up in levels, paradoxes occur. But all of the vows in higher systems transcend and include all of the principles of lower systems. It can get pretty tricky to understand. These are mentioned here because I always like to put the teaching in context from a macro view. Too many people speak from one point of view without disclosing the others, perhaps from lack of knowledge or another reason. You can research any of these paths. For our purposes, we'll think about the lay vows at the personal, physical level of the recovering addict.

- I vow not to harm
- I vow not to lie.

- I vow not to steal.
- I vow not to engage in sexual misconduct.
- I vow to not take intoxicants.

The first four are considered the root vows. To keep discipline for the other vows and to keep our minds clear, we avoid intoxicants. This one is called the Fifth Precept. There are recovery groups that use that as their starting point. It's obvious that a vow of not lying, killing, releasing unchecked anger, stealing or engaging in sexual misconduct might be harder to keep if we're loaded.

If we turn our sobriety into a Dharma practice, every moment that we don't use our drugs of choice, adds merit. Staying sober for the sake of not killing ourselves is fantastic. But what if we stay sober for the benefit of all beings? We stay clear headed, out of our addiction and thus maintain our other vows. Lack of dope means better decisions that lead to lack of anger outbursts, killing, lying, stealing, sexual misconduct—if we're working a recovery program.

> *Staying sober for the sake of not killing ourselves is fantastic. But what if we stay sober for the benefit of all beings?*

I vow not to harm.

Not all Buddhists are pacifists. Historically, some Buddhists have had armies and have gone to war. In one sutra, the Buddha does not condemn the killing of an enemy. That's not the same as condoning it, but it seems that at that time 'to cause harm' with good reason was left as a gray area. Recently some monks have been setting themselves on fire again to protest China's treatment of Tibetans. But for the most part, Buddhism is a pretty pacifist path. On the first sutra level, the vow not to harm is literal and absolute. Do no harm, no matter what. After the introduction of Mayahana teachings, more complexity to the moral dilemma was added with the notion of intention as a factor.

The first vow is pretty simple. On one level, don't cause any being any kind of harm. Try not to punch people in the face or intentionally make them feel bad. Sometimes I'm not so good at this one. I can hurt people's feelings with my tone, my words or even by the types of questions that I ask. As time goes on, I keep trying to apply this principle. Progress happens. The vow is a constant reminder.

On another level, the vow says we don't kill living beings. Does that include plants? No, plants aren't organisms. But plants may contain organisms. The production of plants kills organisms—by the trillions. Apologies to vegetarians, but if we get holy about our vegetarianism you should realize that it is not as pure as you'd like to think. It's better than cruelty of factories that mass-produce meat from livestock, clearly. But consider that we are going to harm beings just by being alive. Our bodies have immune systems. We cause harm intentionally and unintentionally in small and big ways. We do our best. And we purify often. We're on the karmic plane. My teacher always says that in this human dimension, we should work with our circumstances.

The vow does include bugs. I try to never kill bugs—unless they're invading my house. This one can be a real problem. There are ways that teachers explain how to deal with this issue. These include relatively humane methods, blessings, mantras, and rituals. Some teachers say to simply tell the bugs to leave. In our house, we used to have mice because of a large number of bird feeders in the back yard. The mice didn't go away when I asked them to. I put poison outside and humane traps inside. I did this with the same intention and connection as when I eat meat.

I'll explain that in a moment. As for "pests", I don't want to kill these beings, but due to my own limitations, I'm not able to live with them in my home. My intention is not to cause them suffering. My dogs suffer immensely with fleas. We use the flea medications to kill the fleas. It's not 100% in keeping with the first vow. But it is the best I can do while still protecting my dogs. Maybe you'll do better somehow. It's not perfect, but it's different from killing with the intention to cause suffering, followed by the action, then the satisfaction.

Since I started working with these vows, I cannot kill a bug with impunity. I have to make prayers, offerings, and blessings. And I know that there is a connection between that being and myself. It's not arbitrary. The more I practice, the longer I do yoga and follow the path, the more sensitive I become. This is my experience. Yours will vary.

I'm not vegetarian. But I do drink a lot of green smoothies. And I try to keep my meat consumption down. I know that over the years of practice my ability to eat sentient beings has diminished. I can see that one day I'll probably be vegan, but not quite yet. I support humane, locally produced meat over the torture factories. From the sutra view, which is where these vows come from, not killing means restraining ourselves from directly killing? Traditionally, monks who were given meat in their begging bowls were supposed to eat it. This may vary from culture to culture. But Tibetans are not traditionally vegetarian. Many Buddhists are and this has been on the increase in recent years.

When I eat meat, I follow the principles of Ganapuja, which is a tantric practice. In this practice, we create a blessing for the animals that have given their lives. In my mind, it is a very serious commitment to every single being with whom I've shared a meal and have a karmic bond. We already have a karmic bond before the food hits my plate. But instead of continuing the infinite cycle of suffering, with the blessing practice I have a chance to do something different for those beings. This is the attitude of tantra. When I become Buddha, and that will happen, those beings will be connected to me. It's a pretty big burden to think about. And it does take some faith in the tantric path. From the point of view of tantra, we do something with our Ganapuja practice that will eventually help liberate those animals from samsara. If we simply avoid eating meat, we are not directly helping those animals that have already suffered. We are definitely not supporting the killing industry. That's obvious. But does being vegetarian stop the killing? Does our avoidance of a hamburger stop the animals from being reborn in the hell realm of the slaughterhouse? Could we ever convince the entire world to become meat free? Unlikely. So this way we can do something positive. You might have a hard time with this view, and I respect that. But it is the view of the Vajra Masters and one that I work to follow.

Reflections

What are your feelings about eating meat? How do they relate to the first lay vow not to harm?

_____

_____

_____

_____

_____

_____

Many people don't want to talk about this issue. I think the general view of Buddhism is that all Buddhists are or should be vegetarian. That is an incomplete picture, historically and philosophically as well as practically. I avoid direct killing to the best of my ability. I gave up fishing. I'll never go hunting—unless we wind up in a zombie apocalypse—then all bets are off. Besides, zombies are already dead.

From the point of view of Thich Nhat Hanh, we should take the first lay vow further into an engaged Buddhist practice. Here we don't condone killing and vow to not let others kill or cause harm. I'm not so sure on a practical level how this can work. But it's a nice idea. Do we chain ourselves in front of army tanks and nuclear weapons factories?

I do appreciate the view and the activist's intentions. But again, we should follow some logic and practice in a pragmatic way. The idea of being a revolutionary may be sexy until we give it some thought or find ourselves at the wrong end of a pair of handcuffs. I considered myself an activist for a couple of years. It took one protest for me to change my mind. I'm not interested in clashing with police or wearing a hood over my face to create change. The most important changes happen within the individual. **Remember, practical practice**.

Revolutions, televised or not, usually don't change what they intend. Out with the old boss and in with the new boss. The new president loses power, and another dictator takes over. More of the same ensues. Some Buddhist teachers try to use the selling point that Buddha was the ultimate revolutionary and that, as Buddhist practitioners, we can be part of the only revolution that matters. It's a clever idea, and I think what they're trying to say is, "Hey, if you want to be a rebel, join the Buddhist cause." But I don't agree with this, even though I understand where they're coming from.

I feel that practice is more about evolution than revolution. That's how my teacher describes it. We might be tempted to call our practice an inner revolution, but I like to think of it as the inner evolution. We evolve from one state to another, just like societies have evolved from survivalists to mystics, economies, religions, and egalitarians. The difference with Dharma is that the evolution is from the samsaric state of the individual in the human dimension to a Perfectly Enlightened Buddha. It's much more interesting than engaging in arguments for political causes on Facebook, don't you think?

> *...practice is more about evolution than revolution.*

The inner evolution is televised, on the Sony Super Panel of our mind. When I first took this vow my teacher suggested taking the vow at night before going to bed. I will not kill between now and the morning. It may sound too easy or like it's cheating. After all, we're probably not going to kill many beings in our sleep. But when we take the vow and keep the vow, we collect the merit. It's not cheating. It's practice!

There is a practice called the **24 Hour Discipline of the Eight Mahayana Precepts**. Buddhists try to observe these on the Buddhist holiday saka dawa, for example. This is the day of the Buddha's birth, enlightenment and subsequent passing into that state of parinirvana. We keep the vows for one super auspicious day and our merit is exponentially increased.

Lay ordination is where we become Buddhist by taking vows in a formal way. This happens when we go for formal refuge with a monk or group of monks. We get a Buddhist name and are said to be part of the sangha. But I think that as an entry point into the stream of dharma as some would say, the idea of one vow at a time for one hour or one day at a time is practical and useful. This idea works well with our 12-Step motto of one day at a time. We can take one vow at a time for one day at a time, or two, three, four, or five vows. The more we keep a vow, the more power there is in the vow and the more merit we produce, the less we are tempted to break the vows. This is rather scientific. You can try it out for yourself. Merit builds merit. It's like collecting days of sobriety—it usually gets easier to stay sober the longer you are sober.

I very rarely have to kill any bugs. Haven't seen any mice in years. That's the power of vow. In my experience, what they told me is true. If we take the vow it becomes easier to keep the vow. That's the power of vow. But I had to find it out for myself, just as you will. That's the Buddha way. We take the vows, we keep them as perfectly as we can, and we purify daily and retake the vows three times a day or as often as we can.

In addition to not harming others, I'd add that we should not harm ourselves. The vow can become pretty deep if we think about it like this. How many ways can we harm ourselves? We can do some research into exercise, nutrition, and our general psychological health to find out. Perhaps it's easy to abstain from killing beings compared to learning about the ways we cause ourselves harm to our body, energy, and mind.

For people in recovery, this aspect of the vow may be more important than anything else. If we understand karma, namely that we reap what we sow, then harmful thoughts, words or actions to any other being actually harms us, even if the result is not immediate.

The level of physical action is evident, then emotional energy is more subtle and our mental states even more subtle. We have our work cut out for us as meditators as we learn to perceive what's happening on even the most unconscious dimensions of our existence.

If we consider our mental life then the vow practice becomes much more subtle than our physical actions. Any thought that is negative can cause us harm. If we consider our emotions on an energy level then the indulgence of anger, lust, pride, greed, and attachment also cause us harm. In recovery we learn to feel our feelings once we get clean. Then we learn how to gain some emotional maturity where we're less dominated by our feelings.

This is the life of a yogi and of a neo-monastic and a 12-Step Buddhist. It's evolutionary. Integrate, don't separate.

Reflections

_____

_____

_____

_____

_____

_____

_____

_____

_____

_____

Aspects of Self: The Voice of Anger

To find power in vows we can use shadow work. If we ignore the shadow, it creeps up on us. So we give the shadow the power to speak and be heard. Think about validating these voices, instead of pretending they don't exist and shutting them down. They do exist. The shadow of anger is part of the survival mechanism of our DNA. The sense of "kill or be killed" goes back through trillions of incarnations—back to the beginningless beginning. The voice is old. It knows a few tricks. It's best to respect that. Don't think you can outsmart it with a vow. We need to collaborate with this aspect of ourselves.

Does that mean we're making a Deal with the Devil? No more than any other time when we give in to the deepest drives in our minds. We're all Yin and Yang, Shiva and Shakti, Yab and Yum, dualistic—of two minds. In fact, it's not quite that simple. It's my view that we're made up of many minds. The good news is that we can use this practice to achieve a little balance.

Sit in quiet meditation in the way that has been described earlier, or another way that you find useful. From this point, consider the Voice of Anger.

What does it want?

_____

_____

_____

How does it see the world?

_____

_____

_____

What are its healthier parts?

_____

_____

_____

Can you find them?

_____

_____

_____

What does it want to tear apart?

_____

_____

_____

In the first person, as the Voice of the Anger, speak your truth to the following questions. Please don't act out on any of the feelings that emerge. The author assumes no responsibility stated or implied to any actions that anyone performs. Perhaps it's best to do these with a therapist or a sponsor. It's not a good idea to do them if you're high, or have serious mental disturbances. Just do your best to get a little insight into yourself, or one of the aspects thereof.

Think about the Voice of the Anger. It wants to tear things up. It has no conscience. It's primal, but not primordial. It feels basic sensations like hot and cold, dark and light, high and low. Though it has been known to collaborate with Intelligence, it doesn't really think as much as it acts on the basis of survival.

"Who are you? (Say it out loud); I am the Voice of the Anger

_____

_____

_____

What are some other names that you might be known by or associated with?

_____

_____

_____

How do you see the world?

_____

_____

_____

What is your vow?

_____

_____

_____

Where are you in the world?

_____

_____

Where do you live in the body?

_____

_____

_____

Do you speak through more than one person?

_____

_____

Are you, the Voice of Anger in this individual, much different than the Voice of Anger throughout history?

_____

_____

What is your job?

_____

_____

_____

How do you help the self?

_____

_____

_____

What happens when you go too far?

_____

_____

_____

What do you need the self to know?

_____

_____

_____

What are your feelings about the vow not to act out with anger or cause harm?

_____

_____

_____

How can we collaborate on the vow not to act out with anger or cause harm?

_____

_____

_____

Thank you for speaking. Please know that you are acknowledged. Please let your energy be a part of the whole without causing harm.

Reflections

_____

_____

_____

_____

_____

_____

_____

Aspects of Self: The Voice of Good

With the awareness and freedom that come about as the result of speaking and connecting to the Voice of Anger, we can further examine the voice that wants to take the vow not to harm. In a sense this is the fundamental voice of Buddhist thought, perhaps of all religions: the Voice of Good. This is the aspect of ourselves who takes care of babies; calls a sick friend; waits for pedestrians and understands dharma; the truths of karma; suffering; the cycle of samsara; the impermanence and false appearance of phenomena; the fantastic opportunity of being human; the possibility of refuge; and the objects and practices of refuge. This is related to the voice of compassion that leads us to take the vow, restores the vow when it's broken, and keeps us going on the path. This voice understands the Voice of the Anger and all of the other archetypes and has compassion for the conditions of suffering and the causes of suffering. Speak from this voice. Let it be strong.

Who are you? (say it out loud, "I am the Voice of Good")

_____

_____

_____

_____

How do you see the world?

_____

_____

_____

What is your job?

_____

_____

_____

_____

How do you help the self?

_____

_____

_____

What do you know about the Voice of the Anger?

_____

_____

_____

_____

What do you want to say to the Voice of the Anger?

_____

_____

_____

_____

What do you need the self to know?

_____

_____

_____

_____

What are your feelings about the vow not to give into anger?

_____

_____

_____

_____

How about the vow not to cause harm?

_____

_____

_____

_____

What is your vow?

_____

_____

_____

_____

In the Voice of Good, speak the vow:

"I vow not to give into anger. I vow not to cause harm to any living beings.

May all the Buddhas and Bodhisattvas of the three times and the ten directions help me keep this vow.

May all beings be free of suffering and the causes of suffering.

May I be part of the solution."

Change the words if you like. They are optional and just a suggestion for your consideration.

I vow not to lie

From the perspective of a monastic, the most serious kind of lie would be to speak falsely of one's spiritual attainment, or to teach a false doctrine to a group of monks. Minor infractions would include not confessing when asked by the monastery abbot if one is free of downfalls. The abbot says, "Are you pure?" and if you say yes and you know you're not, that's major. Since we're considering vows from a layperson's perspective in general and an addict in recovery specifically, we'll have to look at it a little differently.

We talk often about rigorous honesty in the 12-Step rooms. We take steps to uncover the defects of character that keep us out of a recovery mentality. Since we're already trying to live a more honest life in the 12-Step system, it makes sense to add the power of vow to our recovery practice. Remember, we collect more merits when we make and keep vows. If we're already working a program and we don't tap into the power of vows, it's like having money in a bank account that draws .01% interest when we could drop it into a Certificate of Deposit (CD) for a 5% return on investment. Like a CD, there is a penalty for early withdrawal. If we cash out by breaking our vows, we lose more than if we had not taken the vow. Karma works coming and going. Make sense?

> *...we collect more merits when we make and keep vows.*

In a conventional sense, we might think of what we call "cash register honesty" in 12-Step. That means we don't steal things. This is also covered by another vow. But if we take the principle of honesty further, we can explore how we deceive ourselves with subtle untruths. For this reason, it helps to have a sponsor and a home group to help keep us honest.

From a Buddhist view, the real lie is being ignorant of our true Buddha nature. We deny our magnificence constantly. We sell ourselves short, keep the bar too low and have few expectations of greatness. On the other hand, we may be grandiose and prop ourselves up into "prideful balloons" as they say in meetings.

Our consideration as Dharma practitioners includes not lying in any of the obvious ways. It also transcends convention. We get to know who we really aren't when we get sober. And as we delve into Dharma, we begin to see past the ignorance of our egoic delusion, into the essence of our true nature. The self doesn't really exist. It's a composite that we label as a self. We can use the vows, meditations, study and other practices to crack open the ego, and peer into the light of our innate Buddhahood.

As we go. One day at a time. There are many

ways to lie. We might think of a lie as intentionally telling an untruth. We know better. Do we always live up to the standard of being truthful? Few probably do. To say that we knowingly lie to others or ourselves is to assume that we know the full truth. One of the three *kleshas: a poison in Buddhism* is ignorance, alongside attachment and aversion. It's the root of all delusions and the basis for which all suffering arises. In other words, if we knew to the core that we were really Buddhas, we would be free of the sufferings of samsara. Not knowing that, we suffer. In a sense, we're lying to ourselves. But it's not the same as knowing we're lying. We're simply ignorant of the truth.

But truth has many levels. Most of what we know is superficial or theoretical. For example, how many of us can understand the processes of how our cells function? We can study and learn, but how can we observe in real time the systems of our internal

> *As we go. One day at a time.*

bodies? We have to mix some science (confidence through observation and experimentation) and faith just to get through a single day. There's truth that we know, or think we know, and a lot of truth that's implied. This leaves a lot of room for error. Yet how many of us are humble enough to act as if we really don't know as much as we think we do. We should speak our truth, but with a big question mark underlying our words, as opposed to the deep conviction that we-know-because-we-know and everyone else should understand things the way we do.

Remember that we should use "prudence and a careful sense of timing," as well as sensitivity and discretion when it comes to our truth telling. As the ninth step says, we should make amends, except when to do so would injure others or ourselves. In keeping the vow not to lie, we also must keep the vow not to harm in mind. Remember, there's a difference in Buddhist schools of thought on sutra, which is about absolute morality compared to Mahayana sutra, morality motivated by good intention, and tempered with wisdom. In Buddhism, Wisdom is called *prajna: knowledge of the empty nature of phenomenon,* especially the self. We have the wisdom when we understand this emptiness and we have the *upaya: skillful means,* when we work with everything in our lives with the understanding that it's unreal, just like a dream.

If we hold to a rigid ideal that we must always tell the other person the absolute truth no matter what the consequences, then we won't always act with compassion. We should work with our circumstances and learn to meditate deeply on these things before jumping into a monologue with a friend about how much harm we've done behind their back.

We can try to simplify matters by saying that a truth is made up of facts about a person, place or thing, perhaps a situation. If we pretend we know something that we do not know, that would be a lie according to this definition. How about the sins of omission? Someone might say, "Well I never actually said that I didn't cheat on you," in response to their lover's inquisition about fidelity. Is that a lie? We know it is. But ethics are complicated. I'm not pretending to know the right answer for every situation that can ever happen. That would be a lie. But if we look at our truths and untruths with the deeply penetrating eye of a Dharma practitioner, we can make more informed decisions.

You might say that ignorance is bliss or, "I prefer not to know these things about myself or others." Ignorance is not bliss, according to Buddha. Ignorance is suffering. Like the deepest inner voices that we tend to disown pervasive suffering creeps up and lets us know it is there. We should be brave if we're serious about ending suffering. We can continue our research into the nature of our own minds and live our honest truth to the best of our ability, one moment at a time.

Aspects of Self: The Voice of the Liar

Like any vow there is an aspect of us, which lives in opposition. The Liar has an infinite number of ways to deceive, change, avoid, and fade the truth. He may even try to tell you that there is no such thing as "the truth." That is a lie. The Liar will not want to help you keep the vow not to lie. But as the song says, "You can't hide from the truth, because the truth is all there is."

Let's speak as the Voice of the Liar to see if it helps a little in our understanding. Be careful not to think of the opposing voice as the enemy. That's how it looks on the surface level. Remember, no voice is all good or bad. Everything is relative. In order to practice Dharma, we must develop deeper wisdom that gives us insight into the causes and conditions, which give rise to these voices. To develop a non-dual wisdom, we must develop equanimity with both sides of the coin. That's what it means when Buddhists talk about the wisdom of emptiness and the skillful means to work with circumstances. In 12-Step we call this balance. Give the voice of The Liar a moment to speak as a tool to find some of this balance.

Who are you? (Say it out loud, "I am the Voice of the Liar.")

_____

_____

_____

_____

What is a lie?

_____

_____

_____

_____

What is truth?

_____

_____

_____

_____

Who gets to decide which is which?

_____

_____

_____

_____

What is important to you?

_____

_____

_____

_____

What is your vow?

_____

_____

_____

_____

What is your job?

_____

_____

_____

_____

How do you help the self?

_____

_____

_____

_____

What do you know about the Voice of Truth?

_____

_____

_____

_____

What do you want to say to the Voice of Truth?

_____

_____

_____

_____

What do you need the self to know?

_____

_____

_____

What are your feelings about the vow not to cause harm?

_____

_____

_____

Do you feel that if the self takes the vow not to lie, that you'll die?

_____

_____

_____

Aspects of Self: The Voice of Truth

Before speaking as the Voice of Truth, be careful. My old sponsor used to say that people who are convinced that they know the truth are dangerous. Trust yourself to allow this voice to speak. See what you find out. Maybe it'll be interesting. Remember, and I know I say this often, but the voice can speak how it wants to speak. We can let it out through whatever mode of expression it needs. For example, if you do art or play music, ask the Voice of Truth to speak through that medium. Or maybe take an ecstatic dance or hot yoga class and ask the voice to dance through you. You get the point. Keep it open. Let it flow.

Who are you? (Say it out loud, "I am the Voice of
the Truth.")

_____

_____

_____

What are some other names that you might be
known by or associated with?

_____

_____

_____

What is a lie?

_____

_____

_____

What it truth?

_____

_____

_____

Who gets to decide which is which?

_____

_____

_____

What is important to you?

_____

_____

_____

What is your job?

_____

_____

_____

Is it okay to speak the truth even if it harms
others?

_____

_____

_____

How do you keep a balance between truth and
brutal honesty?

_____

_____

_____

How do you help the self?

_____

_____

_____

Is it possible that there is truth in the lies?

_____

_____

_____

What do you, the Voice of Truth, know about the Voice of the Liar?

_____

_____

_____

_____

What do you want to say to the Voice of Liar?

_____

_____

_____

What do you need the Self to know?

_____

_____

_____

What is your vow?

_____

_____

_____

_____

I vow not to steal

The Burmese meditation teacher Mahasi Sayadaw gives a good summary:

> "...taking surreptitiously what belongs to another person without his knowledge .

.. To cheat a buyer using false weights and measures, to fob off a worthless article on a buyer, to sell counterfeit gold and silver, not to pay due wages or conveyance charges or customs or taxes etc., to refuse to repay loans of money or property, or what is entrusted to one's care and to refuse to compensate for any damage or loss for which one is responsible .. . using force to obtain other people's property . .. intimidation and extortion of money or property, excessive and coercive taxation, unlawful confiscation of property for the settlement of debt, court litigation for illegal ownership through false witnesses and false statements."

— Peter Harvey, An Introduction to Buddhist Ethics

This vow is normally understood to mean, "Don't take what is not given to us." Non-stealing is a principle common to every spiritual tradition that I know of. But what does it mean to be a thief? What is the hand that steals really grabbing for? Again, we can skip the obvious. It's clearly bad karma to take things that don't belong to us because it causes suffering to those we take things from. When I think of stealing, I recall what the famous AA speaker, Chuck C, called self-robbery. He said that to the extent that we aren't doing God's will, we're denying our own Divinity and are therefore stealing from ourselves. For the atheists in the crowd, that kind of talk may trigger your defenses. Understandable. But if we think about the idea of self-robbery with a little bit of a Buddhist filter, we can see how it can applies. We all have Buddha nature to the extent that we live outside of this realization, or inside the field of ignorance.

Time may be one of the most important aspects to keep in mind for the vow not to steal. We waste so much of time in this precious human rebirth. My teacher always says, "Time keeps going ahead." As the clock ticks, every moment that we spend in ignorance of our true nature keeps us locked in the cycle of suffering. Yet we can escape. Buddha taught that in many forms and levels. One way that we can look at the vow not to steal is to vow to keep our Dharma practice vigilant, not on occasion, but constantly. We might say something like:

> "I vow not to steal time from myself. Every moment that I spend in distraction, attachment, and aversion keeps me from realizing my Buddha potential."

Another way to look at the vow not to steal is of course not wasting other people's time. We can be mindful and respectful by working efficiently in our communications with them, for example when driving or asking for something. The time concept also applies to guarding and protecting the depletion of our earth. We should take the concept of not taking what isn't given, to notions about guarding the Earth's resources, by recycling, awareness of the use of energy we use, and virtually honoring all of the "green" considerations.

How about emotions? What do we take from others in the way of sympathy, attention, and affection? Anyone who's done a searching and fearless moral inventory (Step 4) has likely touched a nerve about selfishness and self-centeredness. I think this vow is directly related.

As much as we're thinking about ourselves, as most addicts do, we're not considering others. I'm not advocating that we become obsessed with thinking of others to the degree that we aren't taking care of ourselves. That would be more about codependency than the vow of not stealing. But there is plenty we can do to ease the burden of self-obsession, especially when we consider that it detracts from the happiness that others could be feeling. After all, if the self is really empty of inherent existence and only appears to be real, why would I be so self-absorbed as to ignore the happiness of others by taking what is not given? On the Buddhist path of vows, this is a thought that must stay with us as we develop.

Use the voice practices to discover more about the aspects of self that are related to this vow.

Aspects of Self: The Voice of the Thief

We all know what it means to steal. We can gain insight by exploring the mind of the thief as the thief. It's also interesting to explore the motivations for taking what is not given.

Who are you? (say it out loud) "I am the Voice of the Thief."

_____

_____

_____

How do you see the world?

_____

_____

_____

What is your job?

_____

_____

_____

What is your vow?

_____

_____

_____

What kinds of things do you take (material, non-material; emotions, time, energy)?

_____

_____

_____

Do you ever get enough?

_____

_____

_____

What is your relationship to The Addict?

_____

_____

_____

Why do you steal?

_____

_____

_____

What is at the core of your heart, as the Voice of
the Thief?

_____

_____

_____

_____

How does stealing serve the self?

_____

_____

_____

_____

How do you help the self?

_____

_____

_____

_____

What happens when you go too far?

_____

_____

_____

_____

What do you need the self to know?

_____

_____

_____

_____

How can the self help you be fulfilled?

_____

_____

_____

_____

Aspects of Self: The Voice of Generosity

Another way to look at this dynamic could be the voices of the Taker and of the Giver. As always, feel free to modify these practices to meet your needs. In relation to the vow of not stealing, the practice of generosity is the polar opposite of the thief.

There's relative, or conventional generosity, which is our standard idea. When we think of conventional generosity we're usually limited to what we feel is possible. For example, we might think that we can't give what we don't have or that we don't have that much to offer. Addicts may find theirs in the default mode. We might also feel that we're generous, when we're really trying to serve our own underlying motives.

Words are just as generous as gifts.

From the view of a Buddha, being generous may mean something on the material level, or non-material. The practice of generosity has no limits in the absolute sense. When we work with the practices of Perfectly Completed Buddhas, we try to go beyond our conventional limitations by being generous emotionally and materially. Words are just as generous as gifts.

When we speak as the Voice of Generosity, we can open our hearts up. Then it becomes possible to act generously. In Buddhist circles, we often hear the word *dana: meaning generosity.* In that context, or other Dharma settings, we're often asked to give dana, which means money for the teacher. Giving money is an easy way to practice generosity. We can go along a street with homeless people with a roll of quarters in our pocket, dropping some when we feel all right about it. Some people keep a separate wallet just for this purpose.

But we can also give back to the kinds of people we've harmed in the past, perhaps like those on our 9th Step amends list. Some even devote their lives to helping others as a way to stay out of the selfishness of the addict mind. Many in 12-Step circles have various service positions, from greeting new people to chairing committees. For our purposes, let's try to be creative and think outside the 12-Step box. For example, we could consider some ways to practice generosity on the different levels of body, energy, and mind.

Who are you? (Say it out loud, "I am the Voice of Generosity")

_____

_____

_____

How do you see the world?

_____

_____

_____

What is your purpose?

_____

_____

_____

What are some of the ways that you practice generosity on the physical level?

_____

_____

_____

How do you manifest on the emotional and verbal levels?

_____

_____

_____

How are you mentally generous?

_____

_____

_____

What kinds of thoughts do you offer the self?

_____

_____

_____

How do you help the self?

_____

_____

_____

What do you know about the Voice of the Thief?

_____

_____

_____

What do you want to say to the Voice of the Thief?

_____

_____

_____

What do you need the self to know?

_____

_____

_____

What are your feelings about the vow not to steal?

_____

_____

_____

How about the vow not to cause harm?

_____

_____

_____

Could you cause harm by being too generous?

_____

_____

_____

What is your specific vow, as the Voice of Generosity?

_____

_____

_____

I vow not to engage in sexual misconduct

Sexual misconduct in the monastic codes is very strict and more restrictive for women than for men. Something as innocuous as spending time with a male, outside of Dharma teachings, could be seen as a downfall for a nun. The rules were changed to match the householders that didn't want to be monastic but still felt they could be on the path. The vow changed from not having sex or even sexual thoughts to simply not being adulterous. This was sufficient in the traditional and cultural context of the time. Clearly we need an adaptation to apply this vow in our modern lives.

In our present time here in the West, we need ways of applying this vow that make more sense, especially for addicts. Recovery models have their methods of establishing a sexual code of ethics. In the self-inventory process of the 4th Step we're asked to make a list citing where we have been selfish, dishonest or afraid when it came to sex. It's fairly easy to uncover some of these patterns with the help of our sponsor and support group. Many people in 12-Step are quite open about their difficulties with sex and relationships. Yet we tend to see a lot of sick behavior in the rooms. But at least people are open and working on it, presumably.

There are so many versions of relationships now that it would be exclusionary to insist that misconduct means the same thing for everyone. We want the path of liberation to be open to all who seek it, whether or not they can get legally married.

Relationships look different these days than they did in the past. Some people have open relationships, or are into casual sex, while others prefer fidelity and a traditional style of connecting. We should be flexible with ourselves when it comes to setting standards. We cannot impose our standards on anyone else. That's important. If I weren't paying by the word for editing I'd say it again.

It's important to build confidence in our ethical vows. If we basically think of the preceding vows as a code of conduct, we're probably in good shape. If we don't injure our partners, if we practice right speech from the Voices of Truth or Good, exercise sexual generosity,

> *It's not up to anyone else to set the standard of your sexual conduct for you.*

and emotional honesty, we're safer from misconduct. But just as addiction and its voices can operate on subtle levels, we should try to use our discriminating meditative awareness to discover deep places where voices of sexual misconduct operate. It's not up to anyone else to set the standard of your sexual conduct for you. This is a practitioner's choice. In 12-Step language we call this choosing a safe and sound ideal. It's important to be realistic and flexible. Everything changes.

What we're trying to get at in this book are some ways we can explore similar practices to those in a 12-Step program or other system of ethics. The main point of many of these programs that combine ethical and spiritual thinking is to train oneself to be unselfish. Yet sex is a powerful way to practice attachment and addiction. What is called for on moral and spiritual ground is to act with an abundance of more control than those who do not practice a vow. That's got something to do with why we see addicts with long-term clean time, acting out in old ways. Buddhists in recovery have extra tools to be as sexually clean just like they are from other addictions.

Aspects of Self: The Voice of the Prostitute

"None of us thinks kindly of the term 'prostitute,' and yet from this archetype we learn the great gift of never again having to compromise our body, mind, or spirit.... The Prostitute archetype engages lessons in the sale or negotiation of one's integrity or spirit due to fears of physical survival or for financial gain. It activates the aspects of the unconscious that are related to seduction and control, whereby you are as capable of buying a controlling interest in another person as you are of selling your own power. Prostitution should be understood as the selling or selling out of your talents, ideas, and any other expression of the self."

– Carolyn Myss

Sometimes we negotiate, sometimes we cave, and sometimes we sell out completely. As an addict, it's often difficult to navigate the dark waters of low self-esteem. We have to build confidence and a higher image of ourselves in order to work past some of these shadow aspects such as 'The Prostitute.' But remember, that voice is always going to be a part of you. Maybe we can retrain our inner prostitutes like Richard Gere tried to do in Pretty Woman. But instead of becoming a savior for someone who may or may not be responsive, we can work on our own insides for a deeper sense of self-love.

. . . it's often difficult to navigate the dark waters of low self-esteem.

Who are you? (say out loud) I am the Voice of the Prostitute.

_____

_____

_____

What are some other names that you might be known by or associated with?

_____

_____

_____

How do you get by in the world?

_____

_____

_____

What is your job?

_____

_____

_____

What does sex mean to you?

_____

_____

_____

Are you selfish, dishonest or afraid when having sex?

_____

_____

_____

What kinds of things do you trade for sex?

_____

_____

_____

Is using sex the only way that you operate?

_____

_____

_____

What do you give up in trade for things other than sex?

_____

_____

_____

What is your opinion of sexual misconduct?

_____

_____

_____

What are some ways that you operate that don't involve sex?

_____

_____

_____

What function to do serve for the self?

_____

_____

_____

Why does the self need you?

_____

_____

_____

How do you cause the self trouble?

_____

_____

_____

What do you need the self to know about you?

_____

_____

_____

What is your specific vow?

_____

_____

_____

Aspects of Self: The Voice of the Lover

A little different than the voice of the Prostitute, the Lover can be seductive as well as caring, generous, playful, uninhibited, sincere, and honest. The Lover relies on the Voices of Generosity, Truth and Good. The Lover loves to love and loves to give and is emotionally connected to love making and makes love without sex in myriad ways. The lover takes pleasure in the happiness of his or her partner and those around him or her. I think it's interesting to ask the exact same set of questions to the Lover as we did to the Prostitute. Before we get there, let me share a famous and awesome quotation on love from my favorite writer on the subject. This was actually read at my wedding once upon a time. But that's another story...

"When love beckons to you follow him,
Though his ways are hard and steep.
And when his wings enfold you yield to him,
Though the sword hidden among his pinions may wound you.
And when he speaks to you believe in him,
Though his voice may shatter your dreams as the north wind lays waste the garden.
For even as love crowns you so shall he crucify you. Even as he is for your growth so is he for your pruning.

Even as he ascends to your height and caresses your tenderest branches that quiver in the sun,

So shall he descend to your roots and shake them in their clinging to Like sheaves of corn he gathers you unto himself.

He threshes you to make you naked.

He sifts you to free you from your husks.

He grinds you to whiteness.

He kneads you until you are pliant;

And then he assigns you to his sacred fire, that you may become sacred bread for God's sacred feast.

All these things shall love do unto you that you may know the secrets of your heart and in that knowledge become a fragment of Life's heart.

But if in your fear you would seek only love's peace and love's pleasure,

Then it is better for you that you cover your nakedness and pass out of love's threshing-floor,

Into the seasonless world where you shall laugh, but not all of your laughter, and weep, but not all of your tears."

-Kahlil Gibran, the Prophet

Who are you? (Say out loud) I am the Voice of the Lover

_____

_____

_____

What are some other names that you might be known by or associated with?

_____

_____

_____

What does the world look like to you?

_____

_____

_____

What is your current occupation?

_____

_____

_____

What does sex mean to you?

_____

_____

_____

How do you practice love without sex?

_____

_____

_____

What are the different ways that you love?

_____

_____

_____

What is your opinion of sexual misconduct?

_____

_____

_____

What function to do serve for the self?

_____

_____

_____

Why does the self need you?

_____

_____

_____

How do you cause the self trouble?

_____

_____

_____

What do you need the self to know about you?

_____

_____

_____

What is your specific vow, as the Voice of the Lover?

_____

_____

_____

I vow to not take intoxicants

The reason for this one may be obvious to any addict who's tried to get clean. But for the original monks, nuns and lay practitioners who took this vow, it was to keep their minds clear and their judgments on moral ground. We don't have to think very hard about this vow if we're already sober. But what if we're in the stages of pre-recovery or early recovery? How many times have we promised to stop getting high? How many hearts have we broken along the way? We might not have much confidence in the early days of sobriety to make such a vow. In this case we might only be able to stay clean for a moment, an hour, a day at a time—or not at all. We can wait on this one until we get some sobriety under our belt. Speak with your 12-Step sponsor, therapist, or trusted advisor about this idea. The purpose of the vow is to give us power, not to set us up for more heartache. I want you to build confidence.

There may be some difference among addicts as to what constitutes an intoxicant. If we use the definition that an intoxicant is anything that changes our mood, then we'd have to leave out comedy, caffeine, and candy. What about anti-depressants? We all know what our drug of choice is. **I define addiction as any person, process, substance or event that we engage in repeatedly despite negative consequences.** If hanging out at the Laugh Factory seven nights a week keeps you from paying your bills, you might have an addiction problem with comedy. If you can't leave the house without pockets full of candy bars, or a six-pack of Red Bull, then you might need to examine your addictions with those things. Otherwise, we'll stick with the major drugs of choice here. Mine were pot, booze, pills and troubled women, primarily. But I've also developed problematic behaviors around chocolate chip cookies, anger, Breaking Bad, True Blood... collecting Dharma books...so far all of those are "under control." You be the judge of what you're addicted to or intoxicated by. As a yogi and a sober 12-Step Buddhist, I've become much more sensitive over the years. That makes it hard to go full on into new addictions or back into old ones. If I had a drink right now I'd be flat on my face. The road truly does get narrower!

Aspects of Self: The Voice of the Addict

We can hear the voice of the drunk in our heads pretty easily most of the time, can't we? If we attend 12-Step meetings, we hear the war stories from newcomers and old-timers alike. When we speak as the Voice of the Drunk in sobriety, we may surprise ourselves. Let's see what happens.

Hi, Who are you? (say out loud) I am the Voice of the Addict.

Can I buy you a drink, fix, pill or drug?

_____

_____

What's new?

_____

_____

Who are you?

_____

_____

_____

What are some of the other names you've been called?

_____

_____

_____

How do you see your role in the world?

_____

_____

_____

What is your favorite way to get high?

_____

_____

_____

What are some of the methods you have tried?

_____

_____

_____

How do you like this idea of vows and ethical rules?

_____

_____

_____

What kinds of things do you say to the self?

_____

_____

_____

What is the best thing you can do for the self?

_____

_____

_____

How do you harm the self?

_____

_____

_____

What happens when you get too high?

_____

_____

_____

What are some things that you say to the self when she's sober?

_____

_____

_____

What do you need the self to know?

_____

_____

_____

Do you have a personal vow?

_____

_____

_____

Aspects of Self: The Voice of Sobriety

Here we've come to the Voice of Sobriety. This one can take many forms. The voice sounded different in the early days of struggle and uncertainty. Later it becomes more of a rigid mentality in the first few years of clean time. For some, the voice never evolves into a deeper spiritual intuition. In a future work I'll be writing about the Voice of Sobriety and how it might grow into a more spiritual voice over time. One Quaker teaching calls this the still, small voice within. For now, let's think of the Voice of Sobriety as the opposite of the Voice of the Drunk.

I'm in my 16th year sober. I find that sometimes my sober voice is my drunken voice. These days it's more my teacher voice. I teach a lot of yoga, fitness and meditation classes. But it's also been the voice of Depression, Doubt, and Catastrophe—all in sobriety. There may be many facets to what we think of as sobriety, so it makes sense that there would be a range of voices in our heads. Sometimes sobriety is like listening to the Voice of Confidence, sometimes the Voice of Doubt. In fact, it makes sense that the Voice that is Sober would express a wide range of states and moods. But somewhere inside is the base of our sober voice. It's the little spark in us that says, "Hey, let's get to a meeting," or, "Treatment is a good idea. Pack your bag."

We can try to access that sense of sobriety within us with the voice dialogue practice, with our meditations, our vows, our study, and our other recovery related activities. The process is about seeing the similarities and the differences clearly. But it's mostly about learning to integrate all of our aspects into someone who is, **"happily and usefully whole,"** as the AA Twelve Steps and Twelve Traditions state. How amazing is that? We can talk to and through the shadows, the strengths, and weaknesses and learn to embrace the whole self with the equanimity of 'pure vision.'

In tantra, we can do many things to try to approach what is called pure vision. This is the state of one taste, non-duality, or equanimity. In this practice, we learn to integrate all of our aspects; the five poisons (emotions) and the five wisdoms (pure visions) of the Five Buddha Families. This is represented by the symbol of the vajra. In the center of the vajra is a ball, at each end there are two tips with five points each. The ball represents the state *of prajna paramita, the perfection of wisdom.* The wisdom is seeing that everything is nothing. It's all empty. Not empty of Presence. Just empty of concrete substance. This knowledge is what helps us enter into the next stage of practice. We move from renunciation to transformation. The base or essence of our primordial vajra nature is our Buddha nature, or mind of clear light or sky-like mind. It's my feeling that if we can use our Buddhist meditations and other tools, then with our knowledge of the shadows and lights we can learn to integrate more deeply into that Presence, that diamond like, indestructible vajra essence. In that space, everything is pure. There is nothing to accept and nothing to reject. As they say in Tibetan, EMAHO, fantastic!

Who are you? (Say it out loud, "I am the Voice of Sobriety.")

_____

_____

_____

How do you see the world?

_____

_____

_____

What is it like to be sober? How does it feel?

_____

_____

_____

What is your job?

_____

_____

_____

Is sobriety from your drugs of choice enough or do you need more?

_____

_____

_____

What might you need more of?

_____

_____

_____

Do you feel uptight or loose as the Voice of Sobriety?

_____

_____

_____

How do you deal with emotions without your version of the social lubricant?

_____

_____

_____

How do you help the self?

_____

_____

_____

What do you know about the Voice of the Addict?

_____

_____

_____

What do you want to say to the Voice of the Drunk/Addict?

_____

_____

_____

What do you need the self to know?

_____

_____

_____

What are your feelings about the vow not to kill?

_____

_____

_____

How about the vow not to cause harm?

_____

_____

_____

What is your vow, to the self and to all beings?

_____

_____

_____

The Bodhisattva Vow

There is much that can be said about the Bodhisattva vow. There are entire books and long discourses on the subject. In fact, for some traditions the practice of this vow, and the myriad ways to implement its meaning, make up the entire scope of the tradition. I'll mention the essence of it here, for your consideration.

In general, the path of the Bodhisattva is to commit to saving all sentient beings from suffering. There are said to be ten levels, called grounds, of the Bodhisattva path that lead to enlightenment. But the Bodhisattva will not cross over into Buddhahood, no matter how many millions of lifetimes of suffering he may have to endure, until every last sentient being is free from suffering. This path begins in the Mahayana Sutra tradition and crosses over into the Vajrayana Buddhist systems. The methods used to practice this path differ depending on if it's a sutra path or a tantra path using a transformational deity. I spoke in some detail about this in *The 12-Step Buddhist* and on my blogs and as I mentioned, there are a ton of books and teachings on the subject. If we want to apply this high level of intention, we can do it in a simple and effective way.

How to Practice the Bodhisattva Vow

We put our hands together in prayer mudra (hand gesture), facing or visualizing a Buddha, the Refuge Field, altar, stupa, or scripture (our Dharma library for example). With our understanding of karma, samsara, impermanence, the Four Noble Truths, and the precious human rebirth, we make the Bodhisattva Vow:

"May I achieve total liberation for the benefit of all suffering beings."

Some people think that it doesn't make much sense to try to save all beings. We can't really save each other on the ultimate level. So why try? Because we can help each other—indeterminately. Just like we can, and do hurt each other indeterminately. We're all responsible for our own karma. And maybe our karma is such that we can get some help from Buddhas, Bodhisattvas, and other benevolent beings on the path. Perhaps with our accumulation of merits, we can generate circumstances favorable to receiving such help. If we have no merits, what can we expect? So we have to create some merits. We do this with our practice. If we think about the context of endless samsara with infinite sufferings, it makes sense that development into that stage may take some time and effort. But it's well worth it!

Purification: Cleaning Up Our Act

What is purification? There aren't many detailed explanations about the actual mechanism of purification in terms of how it works or why it works. I recall asking a nun about this on retreat once. She'd done many three month long Vajrasattva purification retreats where they complete 100,000 recitations of the mantra. She didn't have an answer about how it worked but she was convinced that it worked.

In my view, purification is the neutralizing of negative potentialities. When we perform actions, we sow seeds. The potency of these seeds is determined as I mentioned earlier by our intentions, actions and satisfactions. The seeds can sprout when we have secondary causes. If I've sown the seeds of anger with a lot of energy, then those potentialities lie at the ready in my mind stream. When a secondary cause comes up, some trigger like someone crashing my boundaries, this situation provides the secondary cause for the seed to ripen and bear fruit. It may, or may not happen, so the time and exact level of outcome is unknown.

But according to the laws of karma, an outcome is guaranteed—eventually. That's the sense I have of the general dynamics of karma.

Purification is, in a sense, magic. Most teachers don't speak of tantric practice this way, but that's what it is. It's not far off from a stretch really. After all, what is prayer or belief in a higher power, but a form of wonder? What is our life if not enchanted? What is art, or love, or a summer day? It's all a magic light show.

The power of Buddha blessings purifies negative karma. The seeds become neutralized so they can't ripen, even with sunshine. We imagine that all of our karma from beginningless past lives is purified when we practice Vajrasattva's 100 Syllable Mantra. One sticking point to this is that if all of our karma has been purified, why do we not become enlightened after doing the practice? Who knows, maybe we will. But most of us need to keep practicing because negative karmas are infinite. As we purify, we remove obstacles to our own realization and create experiences that add confidence to our practice and our journey. There are levels of *siddhis: attainments*. To obtain siddhis we need to meditate, study, practice and purify. All of these skills help develop our special insight to the extent that our intention to become a fully completed Buddha actually happens.

The two practices that follow are from the Mahayana. The sutra recitation is from the sutra school where renunciation is the principle. The Vajrasattva practice with the Four Opponent Powers is a Tantric practice from the Vajrayana School. From a Zen or another non-dual perspective, some would say that just sitting is purification. It works if we work it.

How to Practice Purification

Find a comfortable spot. Do some breath work. Set your intention. Perhaps do a little silent meditation with your chosen object of refuge. Then recite the following excerpt from the Sutra of Golden Light. Another option would be to do the Vajrasattva recitation, which follows. See the "Daily Practice Guide" below for options on how to configure your practice sessions based on the time available and your needs. As I've been saying, if you're the kind of person that needs structure, you can decide on your practice and do it that way as long as you want to. If you're like me and like to mix it up, that can also keep things fresh.

Excerpt from The King of Glorious Sutras called the "Exalted Sublime Golden Light," a Mahayana Sutra (Sutra of Golden Light), Chapter 4

Chapter 4
Chapter on Confession

One night, without distraction,
I dreamed a vivid dream:

I saw a large and beautiful drum
Filling the world with golden light
And glowing like the sun.
Beaming brightly to all places,
It was seen from ten directions.

Everywhere Buddhas were seated
On thrones of precious lapis
At the foot of jeweled trees
Facing assemblies of many hundreds of thousands.

I saw a form like that of a Brahmin
Fiercely beat upon the drum;
When he struck it,
These verses issued forth:

By the sound of this majestic drum of golden light,
May the suffering of lower migration,
Yama and the poverty of the three realms
Of the triple thousand worlds cease to be.

By the sound of this majestic drum,
May the ignorance of the world be dispelled.
With fears quelled, just as vanquishing sages
are unafraid,
May sentient beings become fearless and brave.

Just as the Omniscient Vanquishing Sage in
the world
Is possessed of every excellence of the aryas,
May countless beings too possess oceans
of qualities,
Concentration and the wings of enlightenment.
By the sound of this majestic drum,

May all beings be endowed with the melody
of Brahma;
May they touch the sublime enlightenment
of Buddhas;
May they turn the virtuous wheel of the Dharma.

Remaining for inconceivable eons,
May they teach the Dharma to guide
migrating beings.
Conquering delusion and overcoming affliction,
May their attachment, hatred and ignorance
be pacified.

May sentient beings who have fallen to
lower migrations,
Whose bodies of bone are alight with
blazing flame,
Hear the speech of this majestic drum;
May the proclamation "Homage to the Tathagata!"
be heard.

In the course of hundreds of births
And tens of thousands of millions of births,
May every being remember their former lives,
Hear these teachings completely
And always recall the vanquishing sages.

By the sound of this majestic drum,
May beings always find the company of Buddhas.
Thoroughly renouncing every harmful act,
May they engage in only virtuous deeds.

For humans, Gods and all creatures,
Whatever thoughts and wishes they have,
May their every wish be totally fulfilled
By the sound of this majestic drum.

For beings born in the most terrible hells,
Bodies alight with blazing flame,
Who wander without aim, bereft of refuge,
filled with grief,
May tormenting fires utterly end.

For those who bear the suffering of humans,
For hell beings, animals and hungry ghosts,
May every suffering be completely dispelled
By the sound of this majestic drum.

For those who are without refuge,
Without base, support or friend,
May I become their supreme refuge,
Their base, their support and friend.

Supreme among bipeds, O Buddhas
Dwelling in worlds of ten directions,
With merciful, compassionate mind,
Please pay attention to me.

O Buddhas possessed of the ten powers:
Those terrible wicked acts
I have committed in the past,
Before your eyes, I confess them all.

Whatever unwholesome deeds I have done:
Not holding parents as parents,
Not holding Buddhas as Buddhas,
Not upholding virtuous deeds;

Whatever unwholesome deeds I have done:
Haughty with the vanity of wealth,
Haughty with age and youthfulness,
Haughty with pride of affluence and class;

Whatever unwholesome deeds I have done
Through harmful thoughts, harmful words,
The thought of harm as harmless
And harmful actions done;

Whatever unwholesome deeds I have done:
Acting with the mind of a child,
A mind dark with ignorance
Or under the sway of a non-virtuous friend;
Greatly charged with emotion,
Discontent with wealth,
Afflicted with depression and malaise
Or under the impulse of frivolous play;

Whatever unwholesome deeds I have done
Through mixing with vile characters of
non-aryas,
Through jealousy and miserliness
And through poverty and guile;

Whatever unwholesome deeds I have done
When poverty came to me,
Fearing loss of the desirable
I prostrate to the Buddhas whose bodies
sparkle gold.

Just as water in the ocean cannot be measured,
And stricken with a dearth of material goods;

Whatever unwholesome deeds I have done
Under the power of a flighty mind,
Ruled by desire and hatred
Or oppressed by hunger and thirst;

Whatever unwholesome deeds I have done
When oppressed by affliction,
For the sake of pursuing women,
Or acquiring food, drink and attire;

Through misdeeds of body, speech and mind,
I have amassed threefold wrong acts.
In these three ways, whatever I have done,
These deeds I confess in full.

Whatever I have done,
Disrespecting Buddhas, the Dharma,
And shravakas too,
These deeds I confess in full.

Actions I have done lacking respect
To pratyekabuddhas,
As well as to bodhisattvas,
These deeds I confess in full.

Disrespect I have shown
To those who preach the Dharma,
Likewise contempt of the Dharma itself,
These deeds I confess in full.

Continually unaware of its benefit,
I have rejected the sublime Dharma;
I have shown unwitting insolence to parents;
These deeds I confess in full.

Childish and veiled by stupidity,
Blind with desire and hatred,
Ignorance, arrogance and pride,
These deeds I confess in full.

Honoring those who possess ten powers,
I shall worship those dwelling in all directions.
I shall deliver sentient beings inhabiting every
realm from all suffering.

I shall place uncountable beings
Upon the bodhisattvas' ten grounds.
Abiding in these ten stages,
May they all become tathagatas.

Until I am capable of freeing them all
From countless oceans of suffering,
For ten million eons I shall strive
For the sake of even one sentient being.

To these sentient beings I shall reveal
This sutra called Sublime Golden Light,
Which rids one of every harmful misdeed
And expounds upon the profound.

Those who for a thousand eons
Committed deadly unwholesome deeds,
By confessing them earnestly once
Through this sutra, all will be purified.

Swiftly and wholly consuming all karmic
obstructions
By making confession through Sublime
Golden Light,
I shall abide on the ten bodhisattva grounds –
Those mines of supreme precious jewels –
That I may shine with a tathagata's marks
and signs
And free beings from the ocean of existence.

Through Buddhas, who are the water of oceans –
Their inconceivable tathataga qualities
Akin to the ocean's profound depth –
I shall evolve into an omniscient being.

Becoming a Buddha, I shall possess ten powers,
Hundreds of thousands of concentrations,
Inconceivable magical mantra incantations,
Enlightenment's seven wings, the five powers
and five forces.

O Buddhas who continually look upon beings,
I request you to gaze intently upon me.
Your compassionate minds always overflowing,
May you hold the remorseful always near.

Due to countless sinful actions
Performed in hundreds of eons past,
My mind is pierced and stricken with grief,
Wretchedness, sorrow and fear.

Solemnly fearing unwholesome deeds,
I shall always keep my mind modest.
Wherever I commit the smallest action,
I will not succumb to frivolous excitement.

Since Buddhas are compassionate
And dispel the fright of all beings,
I entreat them to hold the remorseful fast
And free us from every fear.

May the tathagatas keep at bay
My negative karma and emotion.
May the Buddhas always bathe me
With the water of their compassion.

I confess all unwholesome deeds:
Whatever I have done in the past,
Whatever is done in the present,
These deeds I confess in full.

I shall not conceal or hide
Harmful actions I have done.
In future times I shall refrain
From deeds that render me full of shame.

Three actions of the body,
Fourfold of the voice,
Threefold of the mind,
These deeds I confess in full.

Actions I have done through body and speech,
Clearly impelled by the mind,
Those tenfold actions I accomplished,
These deeds I confess in full.

Renouncing the ten unwholesome deeds
And cultivating those ten which are moral,
I will come to abide on the ten grounds
And acquire the Buddhas' ten great powers.

Every unwholesome deed I have done
That leads to unwanted results,
In the presence of the Buddhas,
These deeds I confess in full.

In the wholesome virtuous deeds
Of all those dwelling in Jambudvipa,
And those living in other worlds too,
In these deeds, I rejoice.

Likewise, whatever merit I have gathered
Through body, speech and mind,
By the force of this virtue's ripening effect,
May supreme enlightenment be attained.

Deeds committed on samsara's precarious wheel,
Those actions influenced by a childish mind,
Approaching the presence of the peerless
ten powers,
All these deeds, I confess individually.
Through feeble birth, feeble existence,
Feeble world and feeble volatile mind,
Multitudes of physical actions,
This mass of evil deeds, I confess in full.

Wretched with delusion of the childish and foolish,
Wretched through association with
non-virtuous friends,
Wretched with existence, wretched with desire,
Wretched with hatred, wretched with ignorance,
Wretched with fatigue, wretched with time,
And wretched in accomplishing virtue,
I approach the incomparable conquerors
And confess all negative deeds individually.

I prostrate to the Buddhas, oceans of virtue,
Golden like Mount Sumeru.
Going for refuge, I bow my head
In prostration to the golden conquerors.

Their compassionate light dispels the double
mantle of darkness;
Buddhas are suns, blazing glory, splendor
and renown.
Golden in color, eyes fine as pure, faultless lapis,
They glow with the glitter of pure gold.

Their exquisite and beautiful limbs are
Utterly flawless and perfectly formed;
From pristine limbs, the Buddhas' sun
Radiates shafts of golden light.

Consumed by the flame of negative passion,
Sentient beings blaze like fire;
They are refreshed and soothed
By the moon-like light of Buddhas.

Thirty-two major marks render their senses
exquisitely refined;
Their awe-inspiring limbs are graced by eighty
minor signs.
Filled with merit and glory, like splendid rays of
spinning light,
They orbit as does the sun in the darkness of the
triple realms.

Pure as lapis with an array of rich color,
Exquisitely adorned by myriad webs of light,
Your limbs resemble the crystal, silver and
crimson of dawn;
Like the sun, O sages, you are enchantingly
glorious!

For those fallen into the great river of cyclic
existence,
Tossed amidst crushing waves of sorrow
and death,
May abundant immense rays of the sun that
is the Tathagata
Deplete the ocean of samsara, violent and cruel.

With limbs shining brightly, the color of gold,
They are wisdom's source, peerless among the
three realms;
Their limbs are adorned with intensely charm
Just as dust on the earth is utterly without end,
Just as Mount Sumeru possesses matchless stone
And the edge of space is infinitely unknown,
Likewise, the virtues of Buddhas are limitless.
If sentient beings took the measure of their
qualities
And for countless eons reflected upon them,
Still the extent of their virtue could not be seen.

If counted for eons, one may possibly know
Water droplets at hair ends,
Or particles of the earth's mountains, oceans
and rocks,
But not the limit of Buddhas' virtue.

May sentient beings evolve into such Buddhas,
Graced with virtue, color, fame and renown,
Their bodies embellished with major marks
of goodness
And the sublime eighty minor signs.

Through these virtuous actions,
I shall soon become a Buddha on this earth.
Preaching the doctrine that guides the world,
I shall free beings forever afflicted by suffering.

I shall triumph over Mara with his army
and might.
I shall turn the wheel of virtuous Dharma.
Abiding for inconceivable eons, I shall satisfy
Sentient beings with the water of Dharma's nectar.

Just as conquerors of the past completed
six perfections,
These perfections I too shall fully achieve.
My ignorance, hatred and desire pacified,
I shall conquer delusion and dispel pain.

I shall always remember my former births,
Hundreds of existences and ten millions
of lives.
Always recalling the vanquishing sages,
I shall listen to their teachings in full.

Through these virtuous actions,
I shall always find the company of Buddhas;
Accomplishing virtue, the source of every excellence,
I shall thoroughly renounce unwholesome deeds.

May the creatures of samsara's various realms
Be at peace, without the misery of their worlds.
May beings who lack sense faculties or hold
defective ones,
Be endowed with powers complete.

For beings feeble in body, afflicted with disease
And in all ten directions devoid of defense,
May they swiftly be free of their ailments,
Obtain perfect senses, strength and good health.
For those imperiled by threats and death from
kings or thugs,
Tormented by numerous hundreds of afflictions,
May these beings – wretched, weak with sorrow –
Be free from hundreds of horrific fears.

For those who are tortured, bound and beaten,
Distressed by passion or captured by delusion,

May these beings – fearful, faced with sorrow –
Be freed from the shackles of bondage.

May those who are beaten find freedom
from beating.
May those facing murder be endowed with life.
May those who are feeble be without fear.
May beings tortured by hunger, craving and thirst,
Immediately find a wealth of food and drink.

May the blind see an abundance of forms
And the deaf hear captivating sounds.
May the naked find plentiful attire
And the poor find mines of treasure.
Through wealth of riches, grain and jewels,
May beings be endowed with serenity and joy.

May no being face the pain of affliction.
May all beings be attractive and handsome.
Endowed with exquisite, beautiful,
auspicious forms,
May every life be replete with infinite joy.

As soon as they wish, may there immediately be
Food, drink, great affluence and merit,
Large drums, lutes and piwang,
Springs, pools, water holes and ponds
Imbued with blue and golden lotuses;
Likewise, may they receive at once
Food, drink, clothing and wealth,
Gems like lapis, golden ornaments, pearls
and jewels.

May no sound of woe be heard anywhere in
the world

And not one being in poor health be seen.
Instead, may beings have great complexion;
In each other's radiance, may they mutually shine.

Whatever forms of excellence there are in the
human world,
Wherever they are wished for, may these come
to be.
The moment they arise, through the ripening
of virtue,
May the aspirations of sentient beings be fulfilled.
May perfumed incense, garlands and ointments,
Clothing, powder and abundant flowers
Rain down from the trees three times.
Thus may sentient beings be filled with joy.

May they venerate inconceivable tathagatas
In all the ten directions,
Completing bodhisattvas, shravakas,
And likewise, the flawless, pristine Dharma.

May migrating beings avoid the lower realms;
May they go beyond the eight unfortunate states;
May they attain the eight auspicious conditions;
May meetings with Buddhas always be received.

Always born in higher classes,
May beings be replete with wealth and with grain.
For numerous eons, may they be endowed
With great form, renown, complexion and fame.

May all women become like men,
Heroic, learned, lucid and strong.
Endeavoring to complete the six perfections,
May they incessantly strive for enlightenment.

May they come to behold Buddhas in the
ten directions,
Seated at ease upon precious lapis thrones
Under bejeweled exquisite stately trees.
May they hear the Buddhas' Dharma explained.

Unwholesome deeds I have performed
And created in wretched existences past;
May those negative effects which ripen due
to deeds
Be completely extinguished.

May those beings who are tied to existence,
Tightly bound by the rope of the cyclic round,
Unravel their bondage with a wisdom hand
And quickly be freed from all suffering.

Whatever beings here in Jambudvipa
And in other world spheres too
Perform profound virtuous acts,
In these deeds, I rejoice in full.

Through the merit of actions of body, speech
and mind,
Through rejoicing in others' virtue,
May every fruit of my prayers and practice unfold;
May the pristine peerless enlightenment be
attained.

Those who recite this dedication,
Who prostrate and praise with an unsoiled mind,
Always devout and free of stains,
Shall avoid terrible rebirth for sixty eons.

By reciting these prayers in verses,
Men, women, brahmins and royals

Who praise the conquerors with folded hands,
Will remember their births in every life.

They shall receive bodies adorned
With complete limbs and senses, myriad merits
and virtue.
The lord of humans will honor them always;
Such will they be in each place of birth.

Those into whose ears this confession enters,
Have not performed virtue under just one Buddha,
Not two, nor four, nor five, nor ten,
Nor in the presence of merely a thousand Buddhas
have they completed virtue.

This ends the fourth chapter, the "Chapter on
Confession," from the King of Glorious Sutras, the
Sublime Golden Light.

Chapter 4: Confession used with permission from
FPMT Education Services, FPMT Inc. www.fpmt.org

Vajrasattva

Technically, Vajrasattva is a tantric practice. That said, it's widely diffused and has been practiced in the context of sutra teachings. It's actually a little bit of a fusion of sutra and tantra. We haven't discussed much about tantra in this book. I have dealt with the context of tantra in the 12-Step Buddhist and elsewhere. Briefly, tantric practice involves receiving initiation from a Vajra Master who holds the lineage blessings from his or her system. The practices involve energy, breath work, deity yoga, visualization, mantra, mudra, and other ritual practices. Some of the schools of Tibetan Buddhism don't differentiate so much between sutra and tantra practices. One should consult a Lama for more on this subject. There is a lot of information online and in print, but it's best to observe the specific instructions from specific masters on specific practices precisely as they are given.

When an initiation is given, it is assumed, expected, or demanded that practitioners have taken formal Refuge and participate in at least the Lay Vows. Bodhisattva Vows are given, at the level of aspiration, which is more of an introduction, or at full power. Following those preliminaries, Tantric Vows are given during the initiation. These are normally done in Tibetan and it's difficult to understand what you're getting at the time unless you really insist on finding out. It's best to commit to the Vajra Master and follow their teachings exactly as they are given. They are affected by the disciple's behavior so they will guide you in how to keep samaya, commitments.

The aim of the Vajrasattva practice is to purify karma for the benefit of all beings. That's why it's part of the Mahayana, with its emphasis on intention and the Bodhisattva Vows. Traditions vary on the specifics of the preliminaries. Some systems require 100,000 recitations of Vajrasattva mantras to satisfy the purification prerequisites to tantric practice. Other systems do not require this. One should always follow the advice of one's Lama in these matters.

For our purposes, we can consider this a sutra practice at the Mahayana level. That means that our intention is to purify our karmic obstacles, those things that stand in the way of our useful-ness to others, for the benefit of all beings. This is the meaning of the Mayahana level and the purpose of the Bodhisattva path. It is also said that one can replace the word Vajrasattva with Tatagatha to make it a purely sutra practice. As far as I'm concerned, it's fine either way. When we receive actual tantric initiations, they often, if not always, include a tantric aspect of the deity Vajrasattva. There are Vajrayana practices for Vajrasattva that involve more than the recitation of the mantra. These are considered the path of Secret Mantra and should be dealt with care-fully and with respect for the teaching and tradition one is involved with.

The ultimate purpose of any of these practices is total realization. Systems, details, and instructions

> *The ultimate purpose of any of these practices is total realization.*

vary, but the goal remains the same. At some point after reciting enough Vajrasattva mantras, we may begin to realize emptiness—that we see the nothing-ness in the everythingness. We feel it, know it, and are no longer deluded by the apparently real mani-festations on the realms of body, speech, and mind.

The realizations are said to move in stages, such that once we attain a certain level of clarity, which we attain because of our practice, we still need to purify on more and more subtle energetic levels. That's why tantric practices exist. We need to purify obscurations and realize reality on levels deeper than the gross, physical layer. It's a little bit of a scary business, because we can go crazy if we open the energetic can of worms. James Low says that the yogic breath (pranayama) practices of ancient India are often referred to as the Royal Road to Insanity. My teacher also cautions us to be very careful with such practices. Nowadays the pranayamas are taught by inexperienced yoga teachers with little if any, knowledge of the dangers or consequences involved. Practitioners beware. Ask questions. Stop if anything makes you feel strange.

In my opinion it's always a good idea to purify, just like it's always a good idea to go to a meeting. If we practice with the intention to benefit all beings, in the context of the Bodhisattva Vows, and take that action and are satisfied with that action, we are set to accumulate zillions of points in cosmic, karmic merit. One can never have too much merit. In fact, it is said that we cannot obtain siddhis without merit. So it's good to purify. And there are many, many ways to do it. You can pick up the FPMT Vajrasattva practice booklet for .99 cents on Amazon, which includes the Four Opponent Powers and special prayers by Lama Zopa Rinpoche. Or visit the Berzin Archives website for detailed explanations, including visualization and pronunciations of the mantra.

The Vajrasattva mantra is provided as a starting point. Your best bet is to go to a Vajra Master and hear the mantra as it is given. This Transmission will give your practice more power. Even seeing it, however, is a cause of liberation. We can ripen that cause with practice. How much practice? Good question. Best get started!

Prostrations

Prostrations are another way to purify. We might put our hands together at the top of our heads, to acknowledge the Guru, then to third eye center, saying "OM." Next we bring our hands to our throat, saying "AH," and finally to our hearts saying "HUM." We can bow our heads, or at the waist, or come to a full prostration on our bellies with arms outstretched over head as we recite the refuge prayer of our choice. Some practitioners do this type of practice on elbow and kneepads for thousands of miles on the way to holy Buddhists' sites. We can also practice mentally, imagining that all beings take refuge with us before Buddha in whatever manifestation we choose, be it a simple male Buddha statue, a Green Tara or a flaming Goddess from the Vajrayana tradition.

Daily Practice Guide

Over the years one question that I get most often is, "How do I practice?" I created a sample meeting format at http://the12stepbuddhist.com, called "How to Create a 12-Step Sangha," http://the12stepbuddhist.com/how-to-start-a-12-step-sangha-meeting which serves that purpose. Several groups around the country have formed using that style of format and, modified it to suit the needs of individual groups. The idea I have for this "Daily Practice Guide" is that it can be used by groups or individuals. It can be mixed or modified. It's really a pretty standard way of organizing practice in Tibetan traditions. As discussed earlier, the general formula for a *tun: sitting practice* in Tibetan Buddhism is something like this:

- Intention
- Refuge
- Meditation
- Purification
- Study
- Dedication

Any of these practices can be done on their own. If you like the breath practice, use it. Otherwise, just breathe mindfully. It'll change everything. Use one of the purifications included or another that you feel attracted to. You're the practitioner, you decide. If you don't like making decisions you can ask a teacher. But then you should do what they say!

Some people prefer to be given instructions for exactly how to do things. There's a tendency to want to do it right. In my opinion, if you're doing any kind of practice, that's a good thing. Right? So, use the "Daily Practice Guide" as it is or modify it to suit your needs. But we have to be careful. If we set ourselves up for too much, we may avoid practice. In other words, try to be flexible. If we feel that we're not meditating if we don't do a full hour on our cushion with our sangha, we may not meditate often. We can take one-minute meditation breaks at any time. We could also do a short refuge prayer whenever we want. Do your work, but be loose, and be free. Don't punish yourself with over ambitious requirements. Like going to the gym, or practicing guitar, a 30-minute session three times a week is better than a two hour session once a week. The work gets into our brain better when practiced more frequently, rather than long intensive meditations.

Intention: it's positive to set intention before literally any action. If we set intention in the context of Dharma practice, some gurus say that we dramatically increase the merits accumulated by the actions. It's especially powerful therefore to set intention before a tun practice.

Refuge: can be practiced alone with one or all three of Buddha, Dharma, and Sangha. In fact, any time we're trying to meditate, study, and purify, we're really taking refuge in the practice.

<u>One Vow at a Time:</u> we can also add the lay vows during a more structured session or at any moment. Feel free to add only one vow at a time, any time, for the duration you want to choose. Be relaxed. Feel free to pull out one vow at a time or go for all of them. Remember you can keep a vow for a moment, minutes, hours or a full 24 hour cycle. Start where you are. Do your best. That's all any of us can ask of ourselves.

<u>Meditation:</u> can be practiced any time, alone or in the context of other practices in any order. You can practice any kind of meditation that suits you. It's all meditation whether we're doing pranayama, purification, study, or contemplation of emptiness.

<u>Purification:</u> should really be practiced in the context of having taken refuge but again, it's up to the practitioner.

<u>Study:</u> we can and should read sacred texts and commentaries whenever possible. That said, it can be helpful to meditate and/ or take refuge before studying.

<u>Dedication:</u> we can dedicate the merits of our practice at the end of a session, the end of the day, after a retreat. If we've forgotten, it's possible to dedicate the merits of all practice that ever preceded the session.

That covers your bases.

We know that we cannot own the Dharma. There is nothing for the self-cherishing "I" to obtain. There is no "I" that can attain anything. We're not going to obtain worldly status or material wealth from the Dharma. If we do, we won't keep it. Real practitioners live this. Real teachers live this. This sense is the knowledge of emptiness or the prajna paramita. Because we know this, or are making efforts to realize it, we practice giving away all of the merits of our practice to the benefit of all sentient beings. We do this with our dedication of merits at the end of any practice or study session.

Intention

May the practice that I do and that all practitioners do be cause for the happiness of all sentient beings, without exception. May all beings be free and rest in the bliss of perfect equanimity.

Pranayama Instructions

I often begin my sitting practice with pranayama but not always. Sometimes I got back to pranayama during a seated meditation as it helps me regroup if I get lost. Over the past 30 years I've done some kind of breathing practice at many different times or when I needed them; before sleep, when on speed, during an anxiety attack, when I'm trying to calm down, or be non-reactive.

Breathe deeply and slowly and completely. After several breaths, fill up a little more than a normal breath. Hold it for a moment, gently. Exhale slowly and completely. Draw the belly into the spine on a slow journey. Press out the exhausted karma from beginningless time. Relax in that empty space for a moment. Breathe in from the deep root at the bottom of the tail bone. After a few breaths like that, begin to constrict the back of the throat slightly. Maintain this as long as you like, perhaps a few breaths or a few minutes. Then relax into regular, organic breathing.

Emptiness

We can use analysis to recognize emptiness or put our minds in the direction of recognizing it. We can try to remember the teachings on emptiness any time we feel attached, afraid or angry.

Notice that there is nothing substantial. Everything is just like a dream. Nothing is as it appears in our mind. Each thought and experience has a cause, which came after a case after a cause on and on into a past without beginning. All phenomenon exist in space. Space is everywhere, between and in and through every molecule of the world, which seems so solid. Cultivate the meditative quality of space. Consider the possibility that the self is just a projection, a dance of lights like the reflection of the moon in a pond. Relax deeply. Retain wakefulness.

Refuge

In the space before me I see my loved ones sitting quietly in meditation. Around them are my dear friends. Beyond them I see many faces that I recognize but have less connection with. Outside that circle are countless strangers. Out at the edge of the refuge field are my enemies or those who caused me harm. Some have appeared on my 4th and 8th step inventories. Some go back to lives I don't recall at the moment. In the sky above us all is a light. In the center of the light is Buddha. Around the Buddha are all of the practitioners of the various lineages with whom I have made connections. The sky is filled with lights, like stars. Each is an enlightened being.

All of these beings are radiating pure light to the Buddha in the center of the refuge field. Those lights bounce off the Buddha down to me. They fill my heart, my head, my being, which is totally empty. Each breath draws in the light and every exhale sends it out to those I love, those I barely know, do not know at all and to those I wish I'd never met. I realize that we all suffer in an infinite cycle of samsara. None of us wants to feel pain, even though at times we may find wisdom from it. All of this has a dream like quality, like a mirage shimmering on the horizon.

From this place of reflection, take refuge in the Teacher, the Teaching and the Community. Repeat three times with or without melody. This can be done silently.

Namo Buddaya
Namo Dharmaya
Namo Sanghaya

The Five Vows

- I vow not to harm.
- I vow not to lie.
- I vow not to take what has not been given.
- I vow not to engage in sexual misconduct.
- I vow to stay clean and sober.

Four Opponent Powers: Refuge, Regret, Recitation, Renunciation

I have meditated on and reflected on the qualities of samsara, that infinite cycle of birth, sickness,
old age and death. It makes sense that the Buddha
taught the truths of suffering, that all suffering
arises from craving and that there is a path to
eradicate suffering. **Everything that arises, arises
from a cause. If I want a different result, I can
create a different cause.** The result I want is the
total liberation of an enlightened Buddha. May this
practice create the cause. I notice that everything is
impermanent. We live in this cycle of samsara but
we have the precious ability to cause happiness for
others. We have
the power to end
suffering. Not to   *Everything that arises,*
do so is a tragedy.
Bugs and fish and   *arises from a cause.*
birds do not have
such power. Yet as humans, we have intelligence
and the faculties to apply Dharma practice. In this
precious human rebirth I rejoice! For these reasons
I take refuge in the Buddha, the Dharma and the
Sangha.

I've fallen short of my chosen ideals for how I
should act according to my own ethics. As an addict
before recovery I did a lot of things I said I'd never
do. I would meet up with people I didn't want to
be like. I compromised my own ethics and nearly
drowned in a sea of self-loathing. Today, I realize
that my principles are my integrity. Yet I'm not
perfect and I've fallen short. As part of my daily
10th Step Inventory, I hereby confess my shortcom-

ings and downfalls. They are. . . . While I realize that guilt and shame can be toxic, I regret that I've caused harm to others and myself. Fueled by this self-honesty and my confidence in Dharma, I will recite the 100-Syllable Mantra once, three times, seven, twenty one or one hundred and eight times.

I picture Guru Vajrasattva sitting over my head. He is white in color, translucent and luminescent. He is seated on a thousand-petal, multi-colored lotus, held up by two majestic snow lions. He wears the Vajra Crown and holds a bell in his right hand and a vajra in the other. His eyes reflect infinite compassion. As I recite the mantra, purifying lights and nectars flow down through the top of my head, filling me with purifying energy, washing away all of the karmic obstacles that obscure pure vision.

Vajrasattva's 100-Syllable Mantra

OM VAJRA-SATTVA SAMAYA MANU-PALAYA,
VAJRA-SATTVA TVENO-PATISHTA,
DRIDHO ME BHAVA,
SUTOSHYO ME BHAVA,
SUPOSHYO ME BHAVA,
ANURAKTO ME BHAVA,
SARVA SIDDHIM ME PRAYACCHA,
SARVA KARMA SUCHA ME,
CHITTAM SHRIYAM KURU HUM,
HA HA HA HA HOH BHAGAVAN,
SARVA TATHAGATA VAJRA,
MA ME MUNCHA,
VAJRI BHAVA,
MAHA-SAMAYA-SATTVA,
AH HUM PHAT.

Having purified, I now renounce all downfalls, character defects, selfishness, self-centeredness and narcissistic behavior. I vow to practice Diligent Dharma day and night, one moment at a time, to the best of my ability. I vow to develop my good qualities, to work my program of recovery every day, and to work for the benefit of others. With that knowledge, I restate my Five Vows:

- I vow not to harm.
- I vow not to lie.
- I vow not to take what has not been given.
- I vow not to engage in sexual misconduct.
- I vow to stay clean and sober.

Study the Teachings

Here you can read any section of a Dharma book or other spiritual teaching or 12-Step literature.

Dedicate

With the power of intention that I set at the beginning of my practice, I know that I've created positive merits for myself. But I know that I have to give it away to keep it. To that end, may all of the benefits of my practice be a cause for liberation for all beings who suffer. May we all be free of suffering and know real happiness.

Commercial

I appreciate you and the time you're taking to read this book. If you find it helpful, please leave a rating and, if possible, review on Amazon, iTunes, Goodreads or wherever you are connected. Tell people about the book. Most places make it easy to gift a copy to someone who needs it. This really helps us authors who are not so famous but try to make a difference in the world. More importantly, spreading the *Dharma: Teachings* brings good *Karma: Cause and Effect.*

"May all beings benefit from our study and practice together."

Bibliography and Resources

Alcoholic Anonymous.Twelve Steps and Twelve Traditions. Alcoholics Anonymous World Services, Inc. Fortieth Edition. 2002.

Berzin Archives
http://www.berzinarchives.com

Buddhaghosa, Bhadantacariya. *The Path of Purification: Visuddhimagga (Vipassana Meditation and the Buddha's Teachings).* Buddhist Publication Society. Kandy, Sri Lanka.September 1, 2003.

Chodron, Pema. *No Time to Lose: A Timely Guide to the Way of the Bodhisattva.* Amazon.com. Kindle edition. September 17,2011.

Dalai Lama.*The Middle Way: Faith Grounded in Reason.* Wisdom Publications. Boston. 2009.

Foundation for the Preservation of the Mahayana Tradition http://www.fpmt.org

Harvey, Peter. *An Introduction to Buddhist Ethics: Foundations, Values and Issues.* Introduction to Religion. Amazon.com. Kindle Edition. July 10, 2000.

Keown, Damien *Buddhist Ethics: A Very Short Introduction.* Amazon.com. Kindle Edition. May 25, 2005.

Kongtrul, Jamgon. *The Treasury Of Knowledge Book 5: Buddhist Ethics: Buddhist Ethics* v. 5. Snow Lions Publications. New York. 1998.

Kurzweil, Ray. *The Singularity Is Near: When Humans Transcend Biology.* Penguin Books. New York. Sep 26, 2006.

Littlejohn, Darren. *The 12-Step Buddhist: Enhance Recovery from Any Addiction.* Amazon.com. Kindle Edition. 2009.

Littlejohn, Darren. *Perfect Practice: How Everyone Can Use Buddhist and Recovery Tools for Greater Happiness.* Amazon.com. Kindle Edition. 2012.

Main, Darren. *Yoga and the Path of the Urban Mystic.* iUniverse, Inc. Lincoln, Nebraska. March 13, 2009

Marich, Jamie. *Trauma and the Twelve Steps A Complete Guide For Enhancing Recovery.* Cornersburg Media.Warren, Ohio. July 13, 2012.

Padmasambhava, Thurman, Robert, et al. *The Tibetan Book of the Dead: The Great Book of Natural Liberation Through Understanding in the Between.* Viking Penguin. 2006

His Holiness Sakya Trizin. 2013. http://www.hhthesakyatrizin.org

Sopa, Geshe. Karma: *Steps on the Path to Enlightenment: A Commentary on Tsongkhapa's Lamrim Chenmo.* Vol 2: Karma. Wisdom Publications. January1, 2005.

Stone, Sidra and Gawain, Shakti. *Embracing Ourselves: The Voice of Dialogue Manual.* New World Library. Nataraj. January 16,1998.

Sutra of Golden Light. Foundations for the Preservation of Mahayana Tradition. 2013

Thamkrabok Monastery
http://www.wat-thamkrabok.org

Vajrasattva   Practice. Lama   Yeshe   Wisdom
Archive. 2013.

Wilber, Ken. *Integral Psychology: Consciousness, Spirit, Psychology, Therapy*. Shambala Publications. Boston and London. 2011.

Williams,   Paul.   *Mahayana   Buddhism: The Doctrinal Foundations*. The Library of Religious Beliefs and Practices Routledge, Taylor and Francis Group. 1989. Amazon.com. Kindle Edition. August 31, 2008.

Vajrapani Institute. http://vajrapani.org

About the Author

Darren Littlejohn is a recovering addict, yoga teacher and Buddhist. He shared his success and program in his book, *The 12-Step Buddhist* (Atria\ Beyond Words 2009). This integrated approach spans nearly three decades of successes, failures, and finally, answers. Darren's books enlighten the inner spirit, educate, open the mind, and fill the heart. The spirituality gained from combining the 12-Step ideas, Buddhism, yoga, and meditation will help everyone heal, no matter what his or her afflictions may be.

Join the mailing list for information on retreats, new books, blogs and more at

http://the12stepbuddhist.com

Here is a sneak peak at Darren Littlejohn's next book coming in 2013-2014:

The 12-Step Yogi

By Darren Littlejohn
Chapter One: Introduction

"Breathe in and touch the sky!
Breathe out and touch the earth!"

Why Yoga?

Yoga is about healing. In my view, deep healing in our world must happen for both addicts and non-addicts; if we as a species and the planet as a whole are to survive and flourish. As a society we have many stress related problems that affect our physical, emotional and mental health. But healing begins with the individual. Every one of us has psychic wounds buried beneath our surface that we may not even know about but affect us nonetheless. Some of these issues live in deep places in our bodies, our energy fields and our psyches. Whether our suffering is in plain sight or dormant beneath the surface, everyone benefits from some deep healing. We are all subject to various illnesses and ailments throughout our lives. Rather than offer a balm to the pains of life, yoga offers us a path to directly experience it, on whatever level of awareness or level of intensity that it arises. We need to feel the pain to heal the pain.

The good news is that we make the choices about how much, how deep, and how often we want to grow our practice. Every day is different, our bodies change-even the two the sides of our body are not symmetrical-and the variables in our lives: diet; sleep; and stress contribute to our practice. Knowing this, we can heal as quickly or slowly as we choose-to a degree. The first step in healing or change is awareness. We'll talk more about this as it relates to the first step in recovery later.

Yoga makes us feel better. One of the yoga practices that I do and teach is called Hatha Yoga, referred to as simply yoga from this point forward, unless otherwise stated. This yoga first and foremost lifts our mood. In fact, a better mood is the effect of yoga that is highly validated in the scientific literature. But there's feeling a little better and there's feeling better like Buddha felt better. Yoga makes me feel better than any drink, drug or other addiction ever has. It's not like we arrive at some peak and stay there. In my experience the spiritual journey is never like that. It's like any trail. It can have hills and valleys and plateaus. But the goal is freedom. Instead of the Full Monty I call it the Full Buddha. That's where we're going. So how do we get there? There are many paths. But what if we're not physically fit? Can we still do yoga? Yep. Keep reading.

Yoga makes us strong. When practiced safely and correctly it tones and strengthens every major muscle group in the body. It also penetrates to deeper layers of soft connective tissue. Ligaments can be lengthened and bone density can increase. Heart size has been known to increase-both the physical muscle and our capacity to love. Sexual vitality increases as does sexual pleasure. A calm sense of awareness permeates our lives when we practice yoga.

Yoga connects us. Most books say that yoga means union. That means it's the union of the smaller sense of self with the Infinite, or Divine Self. In my view, it's even more than that. It's about knowing that there is no separation between us and our real nature. My teacher says there never has been any separation, "since the beginning." Our sense of separateness is an illusion projected by the ego. Not knowing that we're connected to everything and everyone is ignorance, which creates suffering. Cultivating and maintaining the awareness of our connectedness is liberating. That's the prize. We've been sitting on top of the treasure chest of intrinsic freedom forever. But to get it open, we need to understand our situation and develop our capacity to deal with the contents. That means we need to know there's a path that we can step on to, and have some sense of where it leads until eventually, we no longer need any path at all. Yoga methods fully achieve this result.

Yoga is flexible. There are many ways to practice yoga; movement is just one of them. In the West we often mistakenly perceive yoga to be movement related. In the myriad systems of yoga throughout Hinduism, Buddhism and their offshoots, there are also yoga breathing, bathing, eating, meditation, chanting, visualization, and ethical principles. In fact, some teachers have said that real yoga must be practiced in all aspects of one's daily life if its potential is to be reached. People come to yoga class for many reasons: to be fit; lower blood pressure; relax; weight loss; or even to meet people. Maybe the majority of people in yoga classes at Core Power or Bikram aren't looking for enlightenment. But the reason we begin is not important. As sacred texts reveal, it's beginning that matters most:

"By practice, even without understanding, it will be made plain; your body will understand it long before your mind puts words to it. No amount of understanding without practice will work. It is not necessary that knowledge precede experience. Performance will produce knowledge." Shiva, the father of Tantra

My Personal Story

December 4th, 2011

Fourteen years ago today I took what I hoped was my last drink. I once had nearly 10 years of sobriety using 12-Step, counseling and meditation. I relapsed in 1995 and got sober again in 1997. Now, in my fifteenth year clean, I'm still uncovering truths about myself. This time through the process of recovery I became much more involved in Buddhism while maintaining a strong connection with traditional 12-Step and psychotherapy. I still use these tools. But a few years after writing The 12-Step Buddhist, I discovered Hatha Yoga, which is the kind of yoga that uses poses, movement and breathing. It was a perfect fit, so I quickly integrated yoga practice into my recovery program.

Yoga, like the 12 Steps, asks us to peel back the layers of our "self" protection. In yoga and recovery, our repressed "stuff" comes up to the surface when we do the hard work that it takes to overcome limitations. Depending on our situation, these upheavals can be challenging and can leave us discouraged. We often feel that we should be further on down the road than we are, especially after some time has passed. Many people find it difficult to stay sober for extended periods and those who do stay sober often have a difficult time sticking with things that are good for them. For this reason, I feel that it's important to have a roadmap and a guide who knows the road of their own self-discovery. That is what recovery is all about. In 12-Step meetings we say, "You don't have to do it alone," and "More will be revealed." In my opinion, however, sooner or later the work of self-inquiry must be done, whether we're in recovery or not. But yoga can take these ideas to a whole new level. I say this because what you are about to read in this book can help you feel deep joy and yet at the same time it can be very challenging. Somehow we learn to find the joy even in the challenges. But it's best not to do this work alone for many reasons. Objectivity is one. But working with a teacher and a community is an excellent support to our practice. Later, I'll give some advice on how to find and work with a teacher that is right for you.

Some in recovery don't have the interest or ability to go to a deeper level of self-inquiry or spiritual exploration than what is typical in 12-Step communities. In nearly 30 years I've noticed that many people in 12-Step recovery seem reluctant to try new things. It's as if going to meetings is as much commitment as they can muster. There's also a degree of mistrust in spiritual teachers and traditions. I discussed this in The 12-Step Buddhist at some length. Based on experience, I feel that if more addicts engaged in support practices like yoga, there would be more people with long term, quality sobriety. At the same time, if more non-addicts used some tools common in recovery, they'd be happier too. That's the intention behind the 12-Step Yogi. Imagine if someone could lay out a guide to using both the tools of recovery and the power of yoga together. This book is such a guide. You can use it no matter who you are. This book is written in simple terms that anyone can understand

and apply. But since yoga language is Sanskrit, I'll
list these terms after their English equivalent, or
at least my interpretation, for your reference and
to honor the roots of yoga. Recovery and Buddhist
communities have their own language as well so I'll
be using some of those words when needed.

Yoga for Addiction and Other Traumas

Yoga alone can be a valuable tool to help us
feel confident and whole. An important practice
for anyone, yoga is particularly helpful for those of
us who've experienced various kinds of trauma at
some point in our lives. Trauma lies at the root of
addiction. Yoga has helped me immensely to heal
the traumas of addiction. It is an integral part of
my comprehensive, multifaceted recovery program.
In this book you'll learn how to use what is known
about yoga and addiction-even if you're not an
addict-to become "happily and usefully whole" as
we say in 12-Step. Unlike 12-Step, which cautions
newcomers to seek progress not perfection, yoga
has higher goals that lead to a deeper and more
fulfilling freedom.

We will develop skills from recovery that will work
for anyone. The Buddha talked about attachment
as a main cause of suffering. Addiction is on the
same continuum as attachment. I call it attachment
gone wild. It's fair to say that everyone is attached or
addicted to something. Therefore the tools of recovery
apply, whether we use them to free ourselves from
food, oxycodone, alcohol, sex, the internet, or our
thinking patterns. Yoga works extremely well on its
own to free the mind of limitations by teaching us
to let go on deeper levels, *aparigraha: letting go of
attachment* in Sanskrit. The practice of a 12-Step

Yogi combines yoga and 12-Step principles. This integrated practice has even more power than either one on their own, to free us from suffering.

Many people who become addicts have felt inadequate, incompetent, and alienated for much of their lives. Many people feel this way some of the time. But for addicts and others who've experienced trauma, these feelings can lead to problematic and self-destructive behaviors. Recovery from addictions is a difficult path and requires much support. If I look around at people I've known in 12-Step recovery for close to thirty years, I see that many are not very happy or healthy. Many still experience serious difficulties with their weight, for example. It's as if a sign of successful sobriety equates to being a consumer. The longer we're sober, the more stuff-and pounds-we accumulate. I see this as a sign that traditional 12-Step work should be combined with life practices that support and sustain development on all levels. To me, recovery is about self-discovery and yoga is about awareness on physical, emotional, energetic, and mental levels. The three can interplay in amazing ways. We can maximize the benefit when we understand something of the process.

Being in recovery is a spiritual path. In the decades that I've been walking it I've found that the tools of recovery have much in common with the tools of Buddhism, Yoga, and other disciplines. These practices can work well when used alone, but together the results can be very strong medicine. Not everyone needs the strong medicine required for recovery. But everyone benefits from some spiritual work. The beauty of yoga is that we can apply it how and when we choose, as much or as little as we like. Though we use teachers and groups in the process, our development is in our own hands.

What is a Yogi?

"Both yogis and shamans sought to master levels of consciousness that would help them break free from suffering and bring them to a direct and immediate experience of the Divine."
- Alberto Villoldo, Yoga, Power and Spirit

There are many ways one can define being a yogi. Any serious meditator is a yogi. In Tibetan Buddhism a yogi is anyone who has received Tantric teachings from a qualified master and practices those teachings. The highest yoga in Tibetan Buddhism is called Ati Yoga, Ati: highest in Sanskrit. The full expression of Ati Yoga is Buddha. To that end we practice being in the same state as the Buddha. This practice is called Guru Yoga and also has many forms in various traditions. Yet all yoga teachings have the potential to lead to Ati... It depends on how we look at it. It doesn't matter which yoga path the yogi is on, be it movement, meditation or something else. In the end, a yogi is a yogi when that yogi says he is a yogi.

In Hatha yoga, a yogi is anyone who practices yoga with some level of commitment. But we all start in different places. We might attend a weekly gym yoga class or even buy a membership at a yoga studio for more frequent practice. We might use a DVD or online video to get started. My own gym workouts started up again after years of inactivity by using a 10 minute super difficult workout video. Eventually it got me back to the gym. Whatever starts us starts us. Sometimes we begin a practice with no idea of the effect it's going to have on us. Long term, it may change our lives in unexpected ways.

The power of my first experiences with yoga affected me even though I wasn't really aware of it. My first exposure was to the sacred texts, not the physical activity of yoga. I'd read a book on Patanjuli's Yoga Sutras for my philosophy class. I took my first yoga class when I was eighteen at a community college. I was less than committed. My friend and I would get stoned in the parking lot before class. We were so high that during class we fell out of our poses and rolled around on the floor laughing hysterically, tears streaming down our faces. This does not make a teacher happy. But looking back I realize that I used some things from that class for the rest of my life: lengthening the spine; deep breathing; and plow pose. During years of weight lifting I found myself doing yoga stretching in between sets. Sometimes when my shoulders were tight I'd roll into a plow pose. When I felt anxiety I worked with deep breathing. But it would be nearly 30 years before I'd take up a weekly yoga class at the gym and a couple more years before I began a daily yoga practice.

Who's to say when we really become a yogi? We come to yoga for many different reasons. Very few take it as a serious spiritual practice. The practice of yoga, however, occurs on different dimensions and levels within our body, energy, and in our minds. I feel that it affects us deeply no matter how trivial our initial intentions are. I know some business guys who go to yoga to meet girls. But they wind up a couple of years later feeling totally different about life than when they started. It's a journey. That said yoga is a journey that anyone can begin. If we can breathe, we can do yoga. We don't need to be young, flexible or athletic to begin to benefit from yoga. The blessings are available to us all. The path works best if we learn to start where we are and proceed safely in small increments. This book will show you how to do that.

Become a 12-Step Yogi

The path of the 12-Step Yogi is deeper than the average person can bear. We can step on to this path anywhere, but we should understand that it has great potential to become a very profound practice. The beauty in this integrated style of thinking is that anyone can start right where they are. Even if we have no physical ability, we can use our knowledge, breath, and imagination to transform ourselves. The primary requirement for transformation is the desire to make changes. That desire comes from understanding our condition. This book will take you through this process in ways that a beginner can understand and that more seasoned practitioners and teachers can use to deepen their knowledge.

Because this is an integrated approach, we'll be using principals from different principles such as Buddhism. This doesn't mean that we have to be Buddhist. But we can use tools such as mindfulness to help ourselves and others in our development. Integration of Buddhist thought with Hatha yoga and recovery doesn't mean that we mix everything up in a confusing manner. On the contrary, we'll be specific about the similarities and differences.

The 12-Step Yogi teaching and practice is about being and it is about becoming. It's about living in the mindset of yoga and recovery principles as something of a new or neo-monastic path. Don't be alarmed. I won't be asking you to move into a cave or to give up sex—but if you want to, you can.

Traditionally, the more serious spiritual practitioners have become monastics. Since ancient times, monks and nuns have given up worldly comforts to focus full time on spirituality. In Buddhism, where monasticism began, monastics shaved their heads, donned robes in the color of their order, and rejected the world of the "householder." They lived in monasteries, meditation huts, and caves. But that's a pretty rigid lifestyle. Yoga is about flexibility-and not just in our hamstrings.

The 12-Step Yogi can be at least as serious as a monastic. How do you do it? Think of your life as your monastery, your yoga mat as your cave. This is the view of the neo-monastic. We don't have to go anywhere special to get spiritual. We practice where we are and we try to keep our mind on our practice all of the time.

The new monastic takes their spiritual practice seriously. She makes sacrifices to be on the path, ego, pride, and the need to be right. There are several ways to be a yogi and several ways to recover. The 12-Step Yogi is ready to adopt what is needed in the moment to match conditions.

These tools will give you the skills that will enable you to achieve a less rigid, more fluid state of later stage recovery with such benefits as the ability to avoid switching addictions, better emotional health, and a sense of well-being. In addition, this path can help you achieve more happiness, better health, and deeper relationships. And we should know that ultimately a state of enlightenment like the Ancient Yogis and Buddhas is possible.

Stay tuned at http://the12stepyogi.com